NICKEL ECLIPSE

iroquois moon

NATIVE AMERICAN SERIES

*To Be the Main Leaders of Our People: A History of
Minnesota Ojibwe Politics, 1825–1898*
Rebecca Kugel

Indian Summers
Eric Gansworth

The Feathered Heart
Mark Turcotte

Tortured Skins
Maurice Kenny

In the Time of the Present
Maurice Kenny

NICKEL ECLIPSE

iroquois moon

poems and paintings **by Eric Gansworth**

Michigan State University Press
East Lansing

∞ The paper used in this publication meets the minimum requirements of ANSI/NISO Z39.48–1992 (R 1997) (Permanence of Paper).

Michigan State University Press
East Lansing, Michigan 48823-5202

Printed and bound in the United States of America.

06 05 04 03 02 01 00   1 2 3 4 5 6 7

LIBRARY OF CONGRESS CATALOGING-IN-PUBLICATION DATA

Gansworth, Eric L.
Nickel eclipse : Iroquois moon : poems and illustrations / by Eric Gansworth.
    p. cm.—(Native American series)
title: Iroquois moon.
ISBN 0-87013-564-3 (alk. paper)
1. Iroquois Indians—Poetry. 2. Indians of North America—Poetry. I. Title:
Iroquois moon. II. Title. III. Native American series (East Lansing, Mich.)
PS3557.A5196 N54 2000
811'.54—dc21

00-008804

Some poems in this volume, or earlier versions of them, have appeared in the periodicals: *slipstream, phati'tude, Blueline, The Buffalo News, UCLA American Indian Culture and Research Journal,* and *Roadkilbasa;* and in the anthologies: *Children of the Dragonfly, The Second Word Thursdays Anthology,* and *Iroquois Voices, Iroquois Visions.*

The paintings within have been exhibited at the Olean Public Library, Olean, New York, and at the Castellani Art Museum, Niagara University, Niagara Falls, New York.

Book and cover design by Michael J. Brooks

Jacket photo by Sara Morris

Visit Michigan State University Press on the World Wide Web at:
www.msu.edu/unit/msupress

again, for the Bumblebee,
flying smoothly
in ever expanding circles

Contents

The Harvest Moon

The Hunting Moon

The Cold Moon

The Very Cold Moon

Acknowledgments

In first trying to write this page, I had planned to organize the acknowledgments into the categories of personal and professional, but as draft grew into drafts, I found that was not possible—nothing ever being that simple. It has become evident that it is too difficult to trace an idea from germination to fruition. Many influences have certainly found their way into this collection, from Pink Floyd to a powwow T-shirt about which my brother Lee talks incessantly, so who truly can say where ideas come from? One concrete professional debt is owed to Dean R. Snow's historical volume, *The Iroquois*, for valuable perspective, and for structural inspiration.

Other debts are less clear cut in their definition, but an attempt must be made, regardless, and if I have inadvertently left someone out, my apologies. Most significantly, again, thank you to Larry Plant, for everything, but specifically for immeasurable encouragement, and for relentlessly insisting that "poetry and paintings together" would be a natural, regardless of my crabby dismissals, and for the "icons" that started all this. Thank you to Bob Baxter, teacher—in the best sense of the word—for many years of reading, thousands of cups of tea, and though we will never agree on line breaks, I would have never understood poetry in the first place without you. "Who/is it?" Thank you to Denise David, friend, colleague, quick reader (whew!) for reminding me of the importance and beauty of poetry, even on the worst days. Thank you to Bob and Sara Morris, staunch advocates even after that first surprise reading, and also, thank you, Opie, for my poetry mantra in times of desperation, "One tea, two tea/green tea, blue tea," and to Little Miss Science, for the buffalo shoot. Thanks also to the Jupiter II. A tremendous thank you to my family, who can never resist telling a good story, though they have grown considerably less boisterous in my presence, for fear of winding up in another poem.

Thank you to Sarah Kellner, Robert Taylor, and Sandra Olsen, Ph.D., who offered overwhelming opportunities to motivate the completion of the paintings within and without. Thank you to Maurice Kenny, long-time friend and supporter, for reading the earliest draft of this work and offering, as always, advice and encouragement, and to Mark Turcotte, new friend, whose embracing personality and wonderful book, *The Feathered Heart*, served as beautiful inspiration.

Thank you to Bill and Carole Haynes, for welcoming me, during the writing of this book, into their lives and home in the flatlands of Texas—I never thought I would refer to any place other than western New York as "home," until now. Thank you to John Eaves, for broadening my experiences in unexpected ways.

Thank you, finally, to Cliff Trafzer, who has, from the first, walked with a foot firmly in each camp, professional and personal. Your excitement and enthusiasm over my first tentative, general visions of this book spurred me on to complete what I had set out to do. To all, Nyah-Wheh!

Artist's Statement

This collection of poetry is a merging of personal history and cultural history. Structured in part like the alternating colored beads of a wampum belt, patterns emerge from this exploration of contemporary life on an eastern Indian reservation and the sometimes tenuous persistence of a culture after centuries of survival within another, more dominant, culture. The poems, while highly personalized, reflect the tension of speakers surviving within, though never fully of, that larger culture. They are like the darker contrasting beads of the wampum belts—lives formed and meaning defined in their inherent separateness.

The parallel series of narrative paintings through which the poems are organized, concerns the broader history of the Haudenosaunee (Iroquois Confederacy), utilizing the metaphor of the cycle of moons identified in the traditional Haudenosaunee culture's calendar. Additionally, the relationships indigenous communities have had with the United States—from thriving to near extinction and eventually to re-emergence—are symbolized in the progression of an eclipse across the moon. However, another image is superimposed on this moon. This eclipse uses images from the early-twentieth-century five-cent piece as its primary metaphor. The nickel used in this metaphor featured an American Indian profile on its "heads" side, and yet, has come to be virtually the only coin in United States history that is consistently referred to by its "tails" side: the Buffalo Nickel. Here, the image of the buffalo first obscures the Indian from view, and then, as occurs in all eclipses, it eventually passes, and allows the Indian to experience a resurgence.

The identities of the months in the Haudenosaunee calendar are acknowledged by events occurring within the approximate thirty-day cycle, either naturally or formally within the community structure. The parallel series utilizes that structure, literally and metaphorically, chronicling the passage of the moon through the year's events, and also the oddly parallel path of Haudenosaunee history, from its sporadic beginnings, growth, difficult periods, and re-emergence, as well as exploring non-linear, thematically linked sequences of events in the lives of noncontemporary Haudenosaunee people—the Indians thriving, struggling, and ultimately re-emerging.

Symbols common to the culture appear throughout the series: The Three Sisters (Corn, Beans, and Squash), Strawberries, and Green Corn from the ceremonies named for them, and more consistently, wampum beads—within which Haudenosaunee culture is iconographically documented—appear in various incarnations, from the earliest shell groupings, through isolated shaped beads, small strings, and full belt formations. The wampum represents the strength of the identity during each of the historical phases chronicled.

The wampum and the eclipse's progression are the only consistent elements within the paintings, and together, they represent the strengths and difficulties of the identity during each of the historical phases chronicled. The levels of organization and disarray counterbalance one another to suggest the continuity of cohesiveness and trauma—where the moon is least eclipsed the wampum is sporadic, and the places where the wampum has grown most developed and unified, the moon is nearly in full darkness.

NICKEL ECLIPSE

iroquois moon

Nickel Eclipse

Did I tell you my brother is the Man
in the Moon? You wonder how I know
this? I have seen many things
others miss in the flip of a coin.

For example, have you seen
the Monticello nickel?
The spread-eagle quarter?
The flaming torch dime?

Even when the embossed moon presented itself riding
the sky of the silver dollar we ignored
it in favor of a balding man whose corruption will be
acknowledged someday, just a matter of time. It will be
a feature story in a back section of the Sunday
Times, no headlines necessary, why humiliate
the family, I mean, the man's dead and gone, right?
But the moon never fucked with anybody, except
maybe those driven wild in the fullness
of the month, when my brother does not smile
down on them, and leaves them to their own
animal desires, as the tides shift.

I read the Sunday Supplement every week
because Lord knows we need something
to supplement most Sundays and I see
him, between the ads for painless hair
removal systems and those for easy tanning
methods (almost everything coming
in a bottle these days), my brother.

He has the sort of face reservation Indian men
will buy a beer for.
He has the sort of face reservation Indian women
will break and enter for.
He has the sort of face city Indian men
will grow their hair back for.
He has the sort of face city Indian women
will come home to the dark roads for.
He has the sort of face reservation white men
know their wives do not long for.
He has the sort of face reservation white women
hope their men will deliver children for.
He has the sort of face city white women
are willing to pick up a hitchhiker for.
He has the sort of face city white men
are willing to waste the beer in a shattered bottle for.

Maybe you've seen him—though he was born to our mother
in the winter of 1953, after she had fallen
down a flight of stairs escaping the first of her
two housefires while our father made change
with strangers at some bar until his pockets refused
to jingle, the U.S. Treasury knew my brother
was the Man in the Moon, foresaw his coming
earlier in the century, where before Jefferson
and his Greek revival home asserted their dominance
he graced the dully glowing face of
the country's five cent piece.

Sharp and angular, chiseled
onto the flat disc, his eyes
squint so hard as to be
nearly sightless, looking straight
ahead, oblivious to that word hanging
elusively just out of his range:
Liberty.

They must have known what I know, now
what the Sunday throw away paper tells me,
that my brother was to grace the wrong side of
what would become the only coin
in U.S. history to be identified
by its ass end, that the nearly extinct
animal would push its way through a national
consciousness that did not want to see that Indian man
on the face of the coin, a national consciousness
that preferred E Pluribus Unum and The United States
of America to Liberty . . . and justice for all.

The paper tells me I can
for a limited time purchase twenty Buffalo
Nickels at five dollars, and honor
the noble beast so nearly endangered, no dealers
please, only one order per household.

And I run the miles of reservation roads
passing out five dollar bills at every household
in exchange for a promise I know will be kept
to place an order before midnight tonight,
and when the packages arrive, we will sit
and wait for that night we all know
is coming when the full moon rises and my brother
finally smiles down on us, as he emerges
from the buffalo's shadow, while we flip
coins relentlessly into the night, watching and waiting
for the tides to shift again under his influence.

the midwinter moon

Reservation Architects

This poem is for them
because only they
my brothers, sisters
and their extensions
trailing from them
out into the world
know how it is
to be read.

We build it every time

in the failing house of our youth, scented
with propane and frybread
Lysol and shit
dead rats and lilac
kerosene and old carpet
noticed by others, unmistakable
signature of our life, year after year:

1.
in that early first morning greeting
family members tracing their way
through drifted footprints we made
returning home only hours before
expecting to confirm survival for another
twelve months and hungover or not
we deliver as we know we must

in the darkest month when the money went
to heat the house where snow drifted
on the insides of the window sills and we ate
light inventing improbable desperation dishes
which became traditions themselves now
occasionally eating lettuce and mayonnaise sandwiches
to remember the taste of February

2.
in rooms filled with cooking
pots, skinless water drums themselves filling
with thaw from a roof once again defying our attempts
to hold it all together just one more month, but we dance
needing neither utensils nor instruments, the only lines we cross
dividing damaged roads, inviting us ambiguously
below the last layer
of ice cloudy from the storms, to leave or return home

in three-dollar-an-hour ruts where we balance
for area farmers on the still hard edges
tying crusty ancient grape vines
to guide lines, our mother passing
her lunch among us in the warming sun
claiming she is too full, showing
where the shoots will grow if we do it right

in blossoming wild patches of life
where thistle and hollyhock thrive
among the blackened planks and fragmentary
remains, the house we loved and hated
growing less evident with every year's
passing since it burned, the stone driveway
leading to nowhere, waiting

3.
in static filled new summer nights
air too dark to see a hand reaching
listening as the peepers
and the blues and police scanner
collide above us, invisibly cross
a discordant intersection—
competing songs of loneliness

in the hills watching fireworks streak
the night sky with white smoke
against which we all wove big dark
plans of making every single powwow
in New York State and Ontario knowing
even as we cracked the night's last beers
that our real lives would run interference

in air thick with seed and late sunshine
morning dew heavy on aluminum cans
we had abandoned only hours before
in the dark celebrating a last
minute graduation party when the summer
school grades roll in, proving for the moment
we have done it again

4.
in reservation love making
babies retelling the old
rhythmic stories in drafty trailer
bedrooms or on cracked lineless
roads empty bottle mouths smiling
in the moonlight, singing that low
hum across the wet fields of fall corn

in our last bonfire
light of Indian Summer catching
glimpses of red faces under
the harvest moon among the faint
embers, stars for a moment and gone
leaving us only memory woven
into woodsmoke sweetened morning clothes

in the year's first blizzard
whiteness blanketing our roofs nearly
a month earlier than expected, we dig
through cairns caught frozen on the journey
of preservation, piles of drying winter corn
trying to find survival at the core where we
all know it hides waiting for us

1.
in the snow again
watching pale blue steam
rise from the roadside drifts
where we have stopped to piss
and listen as neighbors blast
shotguns ripping through the silent
birth of another year

We build it every time
with the tools at hand.

The Children Shout at My Door But I Am Too Far Away to Hear

It is only her voice
which pulls from me
like cavity riddled wisdom
teeth, the regret that I have
this year missed the passing
on again an increment of our lives
in this place over long
distance lines from a place
she has never been, will never be, having not
seen the ocean in New York, let alone
the Florida coastline where
even through a bad connection
I can hear the winters I endured
as a child running from home
to home on the first
of the year, telling the old
timers refusing to yield
to the Western Calendar
that a new year had ripped
its way into our lives denying
their stubborn refusal, I demanded
offerings from their ovens as
payment with all other reservation
children for our news of the world
and she finishes our present
exchange by promising to freeze some of her
rewards for me, that they will wait
for my return announcing more
time has passed since we lived
in the same place.

Just Lately

I searched
for Leslie Marmon Silko's
Almanac of the Dead
less than a year old
and still hard-spined
with no luck in the city
of Buffalo
      gone by
      gone by

the clerks said
when Momaday also was not there
there, maybe I'd like this
Ken Kesey book just
out with a totem pole on its jacket
Ken trading cukoos for thunderbirds
or *People of the River* brought to you
by Viking
      "in the proud tradition of *Dances With Wolves*"
and noticing the Anglo
looking faces on the jacket
      (characters in buckskin and author with earring, a real '90s
kind of guy)
I had to agree.

So I abandoned the books
for the movies instead
      almost missed *Incident
at Oglala*

Leonard Peltier hidden behind Daniel Day-
Lewis and Clark—the last of their kind
          discovery—it's destiny, man, manifest
but caught
that too. Fenimore Cooper's white Indian gets
major studio treatment
          and Russell Means actually got a
secondary speaking part as the last Mohican of title
and listened
to the dark tribe in the movie
gasp—whites massacred
giggle—Indian got it
          gasp and giggle, gasp and giggle—editorial
"These people are savages"
"This is worse than Social Studies class"
and again, I had to
agree about gasps and giggles—involuntary
escapees from twentieth-century lips
of the dark tribe in the movie
as they lightened with the credits roll
in our five hundredth year of the Lord
in 1992.

Requiem for the Little People

Reservation nights welled black sky ink
seeping over roads and lawns and fields
cut by occasional headlights
angry fireflies racing through the late hours
and far off porches, stars resting low.

Walking those invisible roads unable
even to see the hand I wave before me
the clicking of my bootheels the only proof
to others that I exist, I tread quietly hoping
my passage is not noticed by those we tell stories of.

Believing they wait in the wilderness
lining the roads, I panic at any sound
each twig-snap a warning from the little people, malicious
legendary beings, that they could take me into the woods anytime
they wanted, for trespassing, just a reminder as I walk.

Though no one I know or have even heard of has been taken
I still walk softly on the soot and asphalt, reemerging cocky
only when I have entered the driveway of my destination
where we drink into the night and reminisce, daringly
in the lamplight about other close calls with the little people.

Night streets of Niagara are flooded with light and people
their names and frustrations filling the police blotter randomly
kicking, biting, breaking glass and jaws, competing for publicity
under the blue chemical glare—sodium, electricity and glass humming
monotonously, above the cracked and shattered barfront sidewalks.

In the bright city where the only blackness, blood shining in neon, is wiped away by trespassers remorseful not of their indiscretions, but of being caught, the little people and their threats of an uncivilized life seem almost inviting, though I doubt I would hear the twig snapping amid the shouts if I were to ever venture into the streets.

On the Lack of Needing My Indian Celebrity Sunglasses

So what's it like, anyways
being an Indian after the Last
Mohican has rolled
silent and stoic
across the big screen
and we're done dancing
with wolves and Oscars?

It ain't so
bad, really.
Many people looking
for a little beadwork and turquoise
buckskin and braids fail
to recognize us
even in our Property
of the Cleveland Indians shirts,
goofy grins spread across
the cherry red face
marring our chests
in K-Mart or Ponderosa
allowing us
the freedom to buy
cottony white underwear and dig
into medium rare steaks
just like regular folks,
maybe even catching some Braves
games, grinning ourselves
as we chop the air
with Ted Turner and Jane Fonda
from the cheap seats.

Graham Greene never had it
so good.

the sugar moon

The Final Cut

The neat white border tells me
this photo was taken
in January of 1968

nine months before
my brother's hair had grown
long enough for the school principal
to suspend him
escorting him out
the door past white boys
their hair longer
than his bobbing
with laughter

nine months before
he got a job
on the line and bought
his first ever pair
of new jeans
deciding higher
education was
not for him.

In that moment
his hair was still
blunt from the last time
he let our mother
trim it with the dull scissors
she used to keep us in clothes
longer than our bodies suggested
and he smiled in his too small shirt

listening to the Rolling
Stones' *Between the Buttons*
the record player's pale arm
standing frozen, carving a groove
through the final song, never lifting
playing forever at thirty-three
and a third revolutions per
minute in January
1968.

Reservations Required

I am pissing north
thirty seconds from the border
filtering my one and only
beer into the gravel
lot surrounding his bar
careful the creeping amber
runs nowhere near
my hundred dollar boots
shining in the moonlight.

He steps up and unzips
next to me behind
his establishment and
asks if I remember
the times we walked
here for root beer
and plastic Indians
stiff in their action poses
when the place had been
a small general store
(the closest to the reservation)
that had accepted credit
even from Indians.

"Location is everything,"
he says, shaking off and zipping up.
We watch our silent
foamy trails seep
toward our homeland
in the moonlight.
"It certainly is,"
I reply, heading
to my car and on
into the city
and my new home.

Waiting for You at the Fountain Outside
Lincoln Center

There is something about this place that perpetuates
New York City cabs making me late and for the first time
it isn't my fault, that Indian Time gene woven into
my internal clock, and I think I have missed you
and will have no way of successfully finding you here,
seven generations after my ancestors traded yours
this island for beads and tribal identity for
political correctness and saw
a wall of timbers created to keep us out
turn into a more effective means
street of financial barriers where strings of cut
glass are no longer worth the interest of anyone involved.

We have talked long into the anonymous night
constructing histories and bridges from a mountainside in
Kentucky to a small plot of tribal land, weaving
new DNA, a helix of coaxial cable and fiber optic line,
have seen photos of one another:
you in a Geneva restaurant, disarming
smile wandering across your face as you negotiate
international futures while I stand in front
of an upstate river, promoting my story looking all
"reservation stoic poster boy," as my friends joke
both images digital, encoded translations of rhythmic pulses
on again—off again, coming down the line.

Sunlight failing me, the quad growing thick with ambiguity as I wipe
my glasses, of the fountain mist spraying me with fear I might miss
you in a moment of obscured vision, I circle the fountain watching
every face, seeing you in fifty percent of the white men who enter
my sights, glimpsing you everywhere, emerging from cabs, crossing
against lights, while I inadvertently arrive in family photos that

will develop a world away, my only European trip, when the crimson lights bloom from water, bathing everyone there in red skin, and I worry you won't recognize me, greet the Hispanic or the Asian guy instead, when I see you see me, that smile unmistakable even among the shadows, and you walk straight for me, our hands connect, lock, the circuit begun in the Kentucky hills and reservation woods, complete.

Her Little Red Cabin in the Mountains

Carole has hoped I would write
about this place and the things
it means to her, but I have no way
of knowing how the building speaks
to her, the things it tells her,
the pleasures it brings,
a lifetime of memories grown
in her mind like the trees surrounding
this place, living away the moments
without intent of memory, to discover
one day events from her childhood
have grown roots as sturdy and vital.

She could no more forget the miles
of walks she has taken here than her
own name, as a child and with her own
child, or the way the bears walk
the roads as if the mountain had been
carved for their convenience, the family
landmarks that have been grooved as deeply
and sometimes as harshly as the bears
have gouged trees, but like the trees
she has grown tougher, sturdier
by the unexpected tears we receive
along the way.

As we sit on the sofa, and she
flips glossy pages in family photo
albums of her history, I catch glimpses
of some moments, faces in pictures

significantly absent from pages capturing
later years, voids on the front
deck, like gaps in the wood planks growing
wider as individual boards weather, age,
bow, allow things to pass
on through, remaining whole, strong,
in this place on the mountain where
only shadows of those remaining rest.

Of these things, I can speak: the incomparable
magic of seeing her and Bill making
their way down the airport corridor to greet me
in El Paso—this strange place I have
never been, home for now; eating sandwiches
balanced tenuously on stumps and her laughter
while sticking her feet in the stream at Mescalero
Apache reservation; silent early hours on that same front
deck, drinking coffee as the sun burns morning
chill from the air around us; and I can only hope
my time here was as significant for them as it was
for me, that I might find a place among those glossy pages.

Placemaps

She purchased new placemats
for her table
where he sat
for years marking
progression
with his cribbage board
which now idles
on a shelf
pegless holes
gradually filling
with dust.

In recent years
the placemats
marked the progression
of shaky
unwinning hands
stains growing deeper
and more permanent
with time
so even
bleach could
not deny
the mounting numbers.

The new mats
even with daily use
remain pristine reminders
of everything
he is no longer
there to do

and she gives
them to Goodwill
replacing them with
the old stained maps
to their last
days as husband and wife.

War Pony

From our front lawn
vantage point
we stop silent
snipping old family
gossip to watch more
being born
in my brother's
seventh consecutive car swerving
to a gentle rest
rocking cradled
in the wide State
ditch bordering his place.

"My war pony threw
me," he laments
again at 40 as he had at 21
and we laugh
as we always have
watching him still
alive, squinting and parting
with a wave of
imbalance the dust
which clings
to his braid.

He greets Crazy Horse
in our cooler
passing sweating
brown bottles
to every empty hand

before plunging into
the icy water one
last time for his own.

Wrapping my fingers around
the familiar dusty ghosts
of his, I wonder how
it can still seem
so fresh
after all these times.

the fishing moon

Vulnerability

You tell me as we lie in a bed so dark
the moonlight does not even touch
our eyes with a wavering wink
across the liquid surfaces that you are more
than certain when you are in the shower
I will betray you, the warm comforting baptism
removing my lingering influence and you are left
alone with your most secret
thoughts obscure in steam
on slick tiles.

That I have never grown
accustomed enough to showers that I can think
of anything other than the luxury of them
when I am under the water would reveal too much
of who I am and where I have come from
standing naked before a basinful I had pumped
and heated myself making every swipe
of the washcloth count
evaluating my own reflection growing
more vague in the filmy water of my past.

My Sister's Back Yard

We walk softly in
the June air night
and listen

for Katydids (Jeh-ees` geh-geks)
whose skritches
complain against the dark
damp early summer evening

our soles whisper an invitation
in the grass
a sympathetic ear

but our feet lie
no longer bare
covered in processed fibers
we've been caught
skritchers can tell
sneakers are insincere, sly

a distorted message
calluses' voices denied
or the ingrown toenail
from a frisbee game accident
when we lived in the same house
and chased off the same rats
in the late hours

always seeing ourselves
gliding away in that faded red disc
a space ship in the sun
only to be snatched back at the last second
launched again, and
free for another few seconds.

We haven't played frisbee
in years not even sure if we have one
perhaps tucked away in the garage
or basement.

Would it reach
from my house in the city
to your country estate
both millions of miles from home

and could we even jump to catch it
our feet shrouded as they are.

Mystic Powers (II)

I don't know any Indians
who wear crystals
around their necks or anywhere
else for that matter.
Most medicine bags I've seen
come in the nickel and dime
denominations, having little to do
with the mystical world
Rod Serling told us existed
between the light and the shadow
the black and the white
and more with the magic we pull through
clenched teeth and sharp wind which
is never enough to save us
from even one hot white seed
leaping from the joint burning straight
through our ribbon shirts scarring
the dark flesh beneath.

The Reservation Knows Your Name as Well as I

I remember most the way you kissed
me on the forehead, burning me with desire
that same day my mother edited herself
in mid-sentence, a feat I had not yet seen
in my nine years but the look that had passed
from her to me in the stale dust and sun
filled air of your daughter's city house told me
I should keep my mouth shut of the secret
knowledge that your name had become synonymous
with gossip in the time you had grown decrepit
all those miles away from us, and how my mother tried
so desperately to scrub my forehead clean of your influence
with her own spit in the car we had borrowed to see you
in the first place, that she raised a blister
from which I still carry a muted scar today, but almost as well
I remember how after you died, everyone struck out at night,
stealing dirt from your grave to protect themselves
from you, every morning telling stories of the ways
you changed shape in the dark hours, during your life,
limping in the daylight after mysterious cats had been
shot the night before, unaware your kiss stood out
as clearly on their foreheads as the jars of your death
dirt they kept hidden in bedroom closets and basement cupboards,
burning from the inside.

Fishing with You

Those days we stood
and talked long into the deepening
shadows at sunset and you confessed
you were never much
of a fisherman
as you tangled your line every
few casts into the river spoke
to me of your determination
to find happiness, in your own
dogged fashion, mastering
yourself a hobby
for retirement years before
you plan on needing one to fill
your time.

You said you really didn't care
all that much for the act
itself, needing to give
yourself permission to enjoy
the world around you, river, breeze,
sun as it hit those
clouds and waves in just
the right angles for brilliance
and an invitation
to blindness for someone daring to
stare long enough and hard
enough, defying the sky, and fishing, wrapping
yourself in lures and poles
and convoluted lines seemed to do the trick.

And while I could
blame it on the sun
in its relentlessness,
in all that time
truly I failed to get you
to see that I carried no
pole when I stood with you
there, where the river met
the shore, that for me your
company, the place and the sun's
progression were enough to make
me believe happiness
was attainable, if
only for the moment.

the planting moon

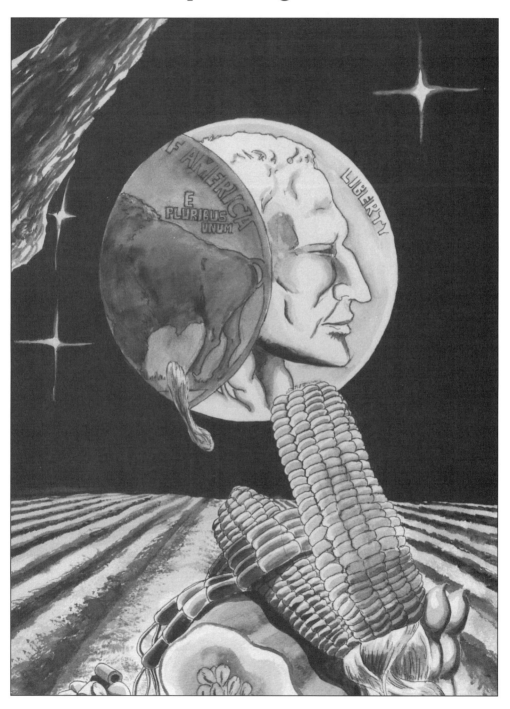

Trading Up

Smooth road bleeds and blends
from the ruts
as we leave the reservation
my visitor from the West,
loose connection to her people is
me in my fast car.

As my arrow blinks East
she notices the Indian Trading Post
hiding beyond her black and shiny bangs
and asks what's in there
perhaps gifts for those in Albuquerque

At my reply, she repeats
certain she has misunderstood
my meaning
"Golden Sneakers?"

I point my arrow West
attempting to clarify
our newly improved homes

so recently with out-
houses and ironhandpumps

but she might as well be right.

I wave to nieces, nephews
cousins, a stray aunt

and gaze at rows of Reeboks, Nikes, British Knights,
cases of 14K gold, only $10.00 a gram,
gram for gram cheaper than other pleasures

and cartons upon cartons
of Hard Packs, Soft Packs, Lights, roll your own
the Marlboro Man glaring beneficently down
surrounded by his hempen halo.

We admire the poster of Graham Greene
hawking Ray-Bans over the counter
and shelves full
of no beadwork, no buckskin, no turquoise
and no silver.

We leave, empty-handed
silent relative waves caress our backs
and we do not speak of our new prosperity
of the guilty pleasures of water pipes
running in the houses, the music
of flushing toilets
as we head East again.

The Gifts of Our Fathers

1.
From your handshake, I feel
the grip of self assurance, a man
confident in his place on this world
as the pressure travels up into my brain
seeping among the grooves, fissures, resting
in that area where the lock of one man's hand
in contact with another is evaluated, the impression
catalogued and here, the connection lasts
a bare moment among the Manhattan crowds
but if I could wish them all away
to another city or planet or universe
where they would blink awake, stunned, removed
I would, for even one more minute of that sensation.

2.
Over dinner, I find myself tracing the arc
of every move your hands make in the moonlight,
large, articulate creatures at the ends
of your arms, dancing their way through
the expert pouring of wine and as you fill
our glasses one more time, you tell me casually, holding
them, palms out into space, that they are your father's
and while I jokingly suggest you should give
them back, in an attempt to erase
the strange look blooming on your face, you ask
me what I remember most about my father, and I
think, as he is still alive, this should be
an odd question, but answer, anyway.

3.
They pretended to search the empty bag that Christmas I was
seven for that last identical box we all recognized
as chocolates even hugged securely in foil holiday wrap
to join the others neatly lined across the dining room
table, the names of all my brothers and sisters printed
on the tags above "From: Dad" in his shaky scrawl but we knew
it would not appear no matter how deep we dug,
and my sister ripped at the package carrying her name, crumpled
the foil from it and tossed the gift unopened back under the tree
saying, trying to make my hands less empty
that the dumb box of dark covered secrets was not worth
the years of shit and yelling and drunken nights,
but I did not care.

4.
In one of six vivid moments you have retained, you
return to fields of tobacco from which you wondered
how you ever escaped, where your father lies enshrouded
in a suit he wears for the first and last time,
but this you only know from comments of others, listening
to a life filling your ears with memories and
observations as foreign to you as this man
when a distant relative approaching you observes
your hands on the edge of the deep grained wood,
touches them, says your father passed on these to you
and glancing at the still extremities whose touch you have not
known in more years than you can remember, you nod
some part of you even believing this.

5.

I stole the discarded shrouds of wrapping
paper from my sister's and from all the others' gifts,
still brilliant and gleaming even abandoned, folded
and pressed them flat, repaired the jagged tears
my siblings had made in their indifference, searched
for signs of his features in my face reflected
in the crinkled and fractured paper, traced
his tentative name pressed into the waxy gift tags, taped
the sheets together—a patchwork—and tucked myself
under them, pretending I recalled a time
he lived with us desperately trying
to remember even a shout of "shut up and go
to sleep. Don't make me come in there."

6.

Over a dark and rich dessert the experience of which
you recommend and have a desire to give to me
I stare at the hearty branches of your life, thick-veined
and impressive, glorious hands you still claim are your father's,
as you use them with power and energy, to tell me
of your brilliant son, who you have trained to eclipse you—the way
you have taught him to call his family, circumventing later regrets,
to recognize his accomplishments and potential, and of the vacation
you spent introducing him to a future he might never have otherwise
discovered and while I have not seen the grooves carved into the hands
of a dead man resting forever in Kentucky I know without looking, by
the grasp of your hand's embrace, and the trails you have already made
in my life, a different truth: no two prints are ever the same.

Stinkpot

We called her,
with her vague peppery smell
 (smudged faced and heavy-haired)
  with her beige turtlenecks
   (used to be white, some year
    on some other body in some nice neighborhood)
    with her gray baggy socks
     snapped elastic hanging from the sides
      (even they not wanting to hug
       her shiny dark shins)
        with her pilled and mended polyester
         stretch pants and cracked plastic Mary Jane shoes
         we had seen at the Salvation Army
          a week before
           all shopping for school clothes
            (passed over on the girls' shelf
             by others knowing not even shiny black electrician's
             tape could hide those cracks from us—we'd sniff
              them out, the scents of fear).

We called her,
from the first day of kindergarten
 (hastily drawing lines and sides from the most shine on shoes
  to the least number of rotting baby teeth)
   from the desks to the north, south, east and west
    (all complaining about being downwind, in the worst place
     possible, some wanting to sit not in alphabetical order
      or if forced, claiming new last names)
       from the school bus panes
        (our fingertips sore and red, having trouble
         getting windows down in time to shout)

We called her,
drawing on the secret trail from our homes
  the commodes of reservation
    life, rank plastic buckets of familial shit

We called her,
even when her cousin who lived next door
  joined us in sniffing the air

        We called her,
          secretly smelling our own thrift shop clothes
            in silent comparison

            We called her,
              buttoning our shirts to that top button
                hiding t-shirts as off-white as her turtlenecks

              We called her,
                in hopes our own hard-living bouquets
                would be carried by her

              We called her,
                so often and so long
                she passed out

Smiling with perfect teeth we denied her on February 14
heart-shaped cards inscribed
        "Happy Valentine's Day

                        Love, Stinkpot."

Baggage Claim

Sixteen years later we each hold something
awkwardly: you, a small brown bag unlike the kind
I am accustomed to your carrying
I, a copy of my first novel
suddenly trying to will our hands empty, feeling
their contents driving deep scars into palms
as we meet again on warm fall
asphalt of our elementary school parking lot
and behind you I see the patch of grass
where that night, at seventeen, it took us
centuries to cross the span
knowing we never had enough to get us
through the night, the last time
entering that field having just
pinched a bag from someone too stoned
to care we were ripping him off, planting
our rumpled founding fathers under his pillow,
improbable seeds for his minimal dreams
of prosperity as he rolled over and gave us
a piece of advice he had never intended: to get
the fuck out, and as we left the wild that night
I just kept going, never stopping, losing
you somewhere along the way.

"That it?" you ask, pointing with your lips
to the bound pages in my hand and I nod
but you do not ask if you are in it, knowing
both answers would require something of you,

and when I point back to your hand, you raise
the package and say: "My kid's birthday, I better
get in there," and I let you go, unaware of even
your child's gender, or what threshold is being
crossed this afternoon, as I embrace that impaired
and inadvertent advice all over again.

Skins at Dinner

That night in October, with Joy in town, we went to the Family
Tree Greek restaurant where your Akwesasne roommate waited
tables and smiled at us talking about the white people surrounding us
in our language, music she never hears, and we contributed to survival
and though my reservation was represented at the table only by me—
an outsider from within—the "real" Tuscaroras too busy braiding corn
for the coming winter, that vague sense of absence was harvested
in burgers and French fries in heavy gravy, and a Muscogee, an
Onondaga, a Lakota, and Mohawks, Cayugas, Senecas, tribal members
from the East Coast to the West, all found home for a couple of hours.

Four Kitchens in the State

While we visit Bill's mother, 89,
living independently in a senior efficiency
complex, her lunch is delivered
by Meals on Wheels and Bill takes it
into her small kitchen, ignoring her
declining his offer, cutting
the entree into manageable sizes
and after she, laughing, warns him
not to steal any of her
ham, she smiles at me and out of his
hearing range, whispers that he needs
to be a good person, a fact
I have known from the first
time we had talked.

After introducing his sister, the flesh
of her hands damp and vivid
yet unblemished by the acids
of potatoes she blinds
in her neat kitchen, Bill guides me
through the cemetery of his family's
town and there, points to a petite
stone that I think is one
the woman we have just seen
has planted for herself, the single year
adorning it, begging for a completion
I can not imagine
anyone planning for
themselves.

They weren't expected
to survive, he says,
arriving early in the middle
of the depression delivered
to a family who could not afford
their futures, or even professional
care for their entrances, he continues,
telling me of the way
his two aunts took turns coaxing
the babies carefully
keeping them warm inside
the old kitchen's wood burning oven
two delicate loaves of bread
rising and falling in the drafty house
but only one remained in this world
as the central Texas sun filled the room
in the winter morning and only then
do I realize the woman
I'd just met had, in the middle
of the night she was born, lost
her twin sister as the moon slowly
finished its lonely arc that first night.

In his kitchen, as I ask after
the ridiculous condiment sandwiches
that seem to be a mainstay
of his diet, vegetable and bread
concoctions of the sort I had grown
used to when the month outlasted
the money back home, when I was
a child and had never even dreamed
a place called Texas existed, we sit
in the growing dark and movement
of a sandstorm blowing across the prairie,

and finally they speak.
Bill and his wife Carole tell me
as we disappear in the shadows
of the day he died for a moment
of how professional care
he could now afford
stood clear and brought him
back with a charge just
this side of the electric chair
and pierced his stubborn and silent chest
then called his wife in pretending
it is natural for hernia patients to code blue
in recovery, but the look
they now share across
the counter in front of me
tells me the truth
of the moment, the fortune
I have been afforded
in finding this new home
so many thousands of miles
from my own.

the strawberry moon

Iroquois Backboard Rebound Song (I)

We finally move as
my nephew's voice usually
clogged with dirty
jokes and the dullness
of nicotine alone
fills the large gymnasium grown
smaller in our adulthood, hitting
the backboard straight on
sliding clean through
the net, stripping itself
as it falls of stock cars
and video games
and all night kegs
and even a brief flirtation
with the Armed Services
along the way
and he doesn't even see
forgetting all
of us sitting, refusing
to take up the song he has
started, smiling only
when his wife,
her shadow having reached out
covering our feet,
leather jacket
and British Knights gleaming
more brilliantly
than the scuffed expanse,
begins the traditional Women's
Shuffle alone over the free
throw line erasing the bars
of red, white, and blue

smoothly inviting us
with the ease of her
natural stride
her feet shifting
back and forth
across the urethane
rewriting history.

Iroquois Backboard Rebound Song (II)

This boy in Reeboks
and hip hop Levi's
Cleveland Indians hat turned
backwards slouches alone
around the gymnasium
periphery pubescently
forgetting his family
a tomcat scouting areas
for singular spray
defying the nature
of the Tuscarora Social
until the Warrior song
drums begin, waking his legs, arms
and he snatches a boy
cousin not a year old
from the sitting mother
and he crosses the floor
married for the moment
to the drums and the song
entering the territory
of the men's world
where they move
with their sons
and the singers stop
only when the dance
is passed on.

Iroquois Backboard Rebound Song (III):
The Art of Guarding

Tomorrow night, the kitchen tables will hold two-dollar frybread,
ten cents extra for butter and room temperature store-brand beverages
at a dollar a can, guarded by a woman who has been doing this for
so long she is able to tell what reservation gossip she heard
on the police scanner, watch the deep fryer, coffeemaker, cashbox,
her grandbabies precious golden frybread themselves in strollers and
her own boys now grown into guards on the main floor, their British
Knights squealing through a failed hook shot racing across the gym
floor, blocking any trespass with the dedication of warriors passing
other teams awaiting their turns spread out along the sides trying to
disguise the benches empty of an interested and fearless audience, the
Clan League games becoming too dangerous for many a bloodsport where
Clan-feuds over the reservation future paths are the real score kept,
the victories counted out in the secret trails of knuckles and elbows,
rusty bloodmarks painted beneath the skin and tallied by teammates
over beers later, adding and subtracting as necessary to keep the
vision alive.

But tonight, the food is brought by all and shared amid the painted
lines, sweat ghosts, skid marks, and those same boys forget last
week's bruises which burrow deeper in their bodies, seeping through
muscle, wrapping around bones, making them stronger as they lift the
lonely and vacant benches from the shadows and carry them out into the
light building two parallel lines where they face one another and
smile and laugh and pass the bag each taking up rattles and drums to
begin again what has continued for at least seven generations
discovering voices their grandfathers left for them and rhythms that
have nothing to do with a lay-up and they go on, waiting for their shy
relations to make the save being the first to enter the red circle
surrounding them and begin the dance in earnest as they know they

must even if it means exposing clumsy, ungraceful steps that have got to start somewhere, and the boys will continue, if necessary, singing and drumming their invitation long into the night, beyond the limits of any whistles or referees or technical overtime constraints—this is no game.

the blueberry moon

My Hair Was Shorter Then

In the months between graduate school
and my first class as instructor,
having never learned
to braid my hair, looking more
like Jerry Garcia than Geronimo
knowing the economics of a pathetic
job market, I cut my losses and hair
for the interview, and passing entered
my 8:00 A.M. American Literature class
where I knew I would be
forced, at Canon point to verbally
grant William Bradford and Jonathan Edwards
their roles as seminal voices in this country's
identity and worrying about how I was
going to do them justice, as it were, tried
breaking the pale ice of an early morning
class with a story of my own, how I had barely made it
to school that morning as an aggressive
driver transforming a left turn lane into a passing
one nearly hit me head on, only to witness
in response a blond haired young man in the front
row look around the room quickly and seeing no
evidence, informed me it had to be one
of those crazy ass drunk Indians from down the road.

Fourteen Years Later I Still Want to
Pick Up the Phone

Though you've been
dead all this time
and I wouldn't know
what to say anyway
the urge to call you comes
most often as I lie
in bed awake during that hour
we all pushed your car
from the deep mud ruts outside
the bar after last call
the Christmas it did not snow
and we rode back to your place
all of your skins as dark
as mine for once, and we all
stripped down to our shorts
and walked our clothes
to your basement washing
machine before you would let us in
and there I was, my briefs glowing
against my brown skin
but we all fell
in that late hour
to the floor
to sleep
too tired
too drunk
to notice
until the morning

when we were
embarrassed to be
exposed as we were
and no matter how clean
my clothes had gotten
in the spin cycle
it would not be enough,
I discovered,
while everyone else attended
your funeral later that new year
none telling me until you were already
digging your own permanent
grooves in the earth.

Walking a Mile in His Wingtips

So when I asked
Great Spirit to grant
that I may
not
criticize my neighbor until
I had walked a mile in
his mocca
Sins,
that sexless
rumble murmur reply "go
for it"
was all
I needed.

All

So I slipped
into some Nunn-
Bushes
and wingtipped my way
on down to Youngstown
      (where real estate value never
      sleeps by the shores of old Niagara,
      and the school jurisdistrict is safely
      out of rage
         of range
         of reservation borders
            and bullets)

And landed, somewhat disheveled
in the living room of a

SUMPTUOUS 3 STOREY RIVERFRONT TUDOR
5 BEDRM. 2 1/2 BATH, WHIRLPOOL
MUST BE SEEN

startled family of four
mystified, sat crosslegged in front of the

REAL HEARTHSTONE FULLY FUNCTIONAL FIREPLACE

immolating marshmallows barely hanging on,
      dangling from stainless steel shish-kabob skewers.
And I said
      "Hey! I like this."
"I really like this."
"Pass me one of them marshmallows."
They did
I squished it through my teeth
savoring the decadence.

This was the good life.

I made them stay
in the kitchen,
at first,
and then
bedroom, laundry room,
utility closet,
garage, storage shed, back yard
      "Damn it! You're spoiling my view!"

but I grew
tired,
just grew
tired of all
All
this moving
So I said to hell with it,
and shot them all

All
waking Youngstownites
never heard gunshots in
Youngstown before
        (none old enough to remember).

And I finished off the night
by the fire
on the shore of old Niagara,
loosening, but
keeping on
the sudden comfort
of my neighbor's
wingtips.

Immersion

That night, as you stood
in the open door
of your car too long
we let in the late,
damp air, allowing it to crawl
through the marrow of our
arms growing impossibly
heavy, with moisture and
cold, I made small
talk to delay your departure,
to be near you, to see
your smile, to revel in the distance
in your Georgia accent, that takes me
from this place I have lived
out my entire life, and though
you wrapped yourself in
a heavy sweatshirt, offering
that you have never acclimated
to the northern atmosphere, I know
it will not warm you, burn off the
history of our lives to the point
of embrace our friendship has not
yet comfortably bridged, and I grasp
your hand and allow you that
graceful exit, listening
to your car's heater
fading into the darkness
my aching arms closed
around me, the cold
sinking deeper.

Spanish Lessons

101

A dark skinned person walking east
on a west Texas street at noon
when shadows are equal regardless
of the directions one's life is taking
at one mile an hour sees a light
skinned person accompanied by another
dark skinned person walking west
at one and a half miles an hour.
At the spot where the two paths bisect
one another, where shadows
merge the first dark skinned
person speaks to the second person
of darker skin, ignoring the light
skinned person, entirely, using
language neither recipient knows.

1. What is the line spoken by the first dark skinned person?
     a.) "What kind of work are you doing for him?"
     b.) "Does he give you a fair wage?"
     c.) "Is he holding immigration over your head?"
     d.) "Is he making you walk that fast?"
     e.) "Why aren't you associating with your own kind?"
     f.) all of the above.
     g.) none of the above.

2. What is the appropriate response from the light skinned person?
     a.) "My friend is Indian."
     b.) "My friend doesn't know Spanish."
     c.) My friend knows Spanish?
     d.) Are they talking about me?
     e.) They are talking about me.

f.) Are they talking shit about me?

g.) They are talking shit about me.

3. What is the appropriate response from the second dark skinned person?

a.) I do not understand you

b.) I do not understand you

c.) I do not understand you

d.) I do not understand you

e.) I do not understand you

f.) all of the above

g.) all of the above

102

It happens early that first
morning I am in west Texas
the air still sharp in the shadows
of garages the doors of which
we anticipate opening, with the others
some smoking, some looking
at the door, willing it to open
early for us, some standing
in the sun, trying to catch
that little bit of warmth it offers
at 8:00 A.M. in this wind.

Most do not look at each other knowing
they are the competition, that once
the door opens, we will all scan quickly
for that discarded item which only we,
our eyes as sharp as a bird of prey's,
recognize for the riches it contains, only
we know how to make those distinctions
of worth and worthlessness
along such fine lines.

Hesitant to break the silence, I whisper
to Bill, asking him what kinds of things
he is looking most for and in my revealing this
collusion, a woman who could have been
from my reservation hisses something
unintelligible to me and as I shake
my head at her, and Bill explains I am
"Indios," her smirk as she stares
at my mustache and goatee, and all
the other ways I do not look
like a photograph by Edward Curtis tells
me she believes I am trying to hide
my Hispanic background, in lies
of reservation poverty and obscene mortality
rates, and I am startled to find someone
who believes she is lower
on the scorn scale than I
have been all my life.

201

What is it that keeps me in
their eyes from having any
connection to my own life?
Am I supposed to grow
my hair back, spontaneously, all
the inches that have been
cut over the last thirty-four
years, meld them back on
and then divide those strands at the center
of my forehead and weave them
into two gleaming boas slithering
across my back, black and shiny
DNA helixes proving who I am?

Should I sneak into the Buffalo
Zoo back home and rip feathers
from rancorous eagles and shove
them into my newly dense hair, hoping
their spines will take root and grow some
tradition just this once for me to stand
tall and proud?

Should I yank the wiry hairs from my face
one by one and cross them into tiny braids
anchoring those feathers, or maybe just cut
deep into my muscles, tease out the strands
of Guanine/Adenine/Thymine/Cytosine
until I find those genes belonging
to that white man who connected with
that Indian woman a couple hundred
years ago, maybe even calling it love
as he slipped it in her, changing all
of our lives from that point on?

And when I find them, should I shake
those nucleotides loose from my body, snap them out
like ticks grown fat in gluttony, set them
to bleed out on this hazy plain in west Texas,
and hope their teeth did not remain imbedded?

And if I did, would my mustache blow
from my face like so much dust, leaving discrete
holes from dead follicles as my skin
darkened and my cheekbones rose like saw
blades under my skin? Would my laughter
dry up and my mouth close frozen in flatline
as a blanket wove itself around me, strand
by strand and Hey! Is that small pox I smell?

202

And what is it that keeps me in
their eyes from having any
connection to your life?

As you and I stand among them and
smile in one another's presence, laughing
and you tirelessly explain I do not
know what they are saying to me, they nod
at me regardless and continue on, trying
to awaken whatever violated part
of me still speaks with theirs, to share
that boundary they are building, even
as they work with you and smile that
different smile which allows us to know
what they are saying without translation.

It seems to have that connection
with you somehow destroys mine
with them, but have they forgotten
that Spanish is as ludicrous coming
from them as English is filtering
through my brain? Can they not see
that my connection to you is no less
tenuous than the one I have to them?

Is it that my skin darkens closer
to their brown than your pink, where
even weathered, you look a little raw
around the edges?

Is it that my beard is unruly, steely
like theirs, that it is so unlike
yours, full, dense, and neatly bordered?

Is it that my conquerors just didn't look
as much like me as theirs did they, that my DNA
is not so color coordinated?

Do these things keep us forever
separated under a west Texas sun?

¿Por Que?

the lost moon

Song for a Snapping Turtle Rattle

1.
She has teeth
remember that she has
teeth.

2.
This is what he does.

3.
He puts in sixteen hour shifts, securing pieces on radiators gliding
ceaselessly across a conveyer belt, ensuring General Motors will
continue to career coolly across this continent occasionally disturbing
the rest of the giant turtle sleeping beneath the layers of crust, rock,
clay, mineral fuels, vast secret reserves of ore, and dirt, where life
thrives secretly, growing in microscopic dances until strong enough to
emerge, or grown so accustomed, lives out entire complicated spans
never seeing the sun, eyes grown vestigial in their lack of finding a soul
in the darkness no human alive has seen, among bones, bones, bones

4.
bones turning from memory
bones turning from flesh
bones turning from satin
bones turning to ash
bones turning to dust
bones turning to stone

5.
bones turning from stone
bones turning from dust
bones turning from ash

bones turning to satin
bones turning to flesh
bones turning to memory

6.

Bones turning up missing from their designated numbers and shelves
in Museum back rooms where they have been hidden by curators who know
they can no longer display them, officially on paper, and in some secret
way, know they would not want their great great great grandparents
unearthed, accused without substantiation of the brutality of
cannibalism as a warrant justifying being dragged under the archival
lighting in the name of historical accuracy, but can not let go
regardless, can not let them go back to the earth they might not even be
able to find, bleached as it has been from their surfaces, stripped from
even the smallest crevices mapping the broad cranium, cradling seven
generations of memories and culture and stories born of an accuracy no
book can match, no matter how many footnotes and references to previous
footnotes are housed within.

7.

Their absence is discovered by the night watchman, who has all the keys
and who has grown over the years tired of looking at everything behind
glass watching for hours on end as nothing moves and will not move, even
if he pretends to close his eyes and watch them through slits sharpened
in their narrow focus, he who knows the combination, was given the
combination, and who entered the back rooms where no tourist is allowed
and that was where he first saw her, the love of his life: Indigenous
Woman, Probably Onondaga, boxed and shelved with a small individual
bowl she, it is theorized, had to use in isolation when she followed the
moon's cycle and a small strip of cloth he strokes even as it flakes
off in his hands and wipes what little memory she has on his security
uniform pants, natural fiber locking with synthetic fiber, burrowing so deep
only dry cleaning fluid will dissolve and release it from his permanent press.

8.

She has a small skull, broad yet graceful and he has for years lifted
her from the box, run his fingers down her weak jaw line, pressed
its grooves back into the skull so he can see her perfect teeth line up
and smile silently at him, has even, after a full sweep to ensure they
were alone, unzipped his uniform pants and slipped his flaccid penis
between her jaws, softly rubbing against those ancient teeth, imagining
what it must have been like when there were lips, soft tissue, a tongue
belonging to Indigenous Woman, Probably Onondaga, closing his eyes
and willing her back long enough to take care of business, and though
he stopped this practice after the story of Jeffrey Dahmer broke,
continued to carry two sets of finger bones, crossing borders with an
eternal peace sign from her in his front pants pockets whenever he
traveled to the Indian casino, rolling her bones for luck before those
on the table, never realizing as he walked away with nothing in his
pockets but those two fingers, that they were also used as a V sign by
someone who had less reason for victory or vengeance than she.

9.

One night when he can contain his loneliness no longer, forcing himself
to forget about that other isolated man, the one archiving his own lack
of connection in neat boxes in Milwaukee long enough to be ready for
her, he discovers her empty box, and plays back hours and hours of
surveillance camera video, until his eyes bleed, burned out
on unsuspicious characters' faces as they stroll by the blank eye, never
even aware, except one man who smiles and shakes a rattle at the camera,
dry Indian corn colliding silently with the empty interior of the
snapping turtle shell like the magnetized particles shifting across the
tape documenting his visit, and he is dark enough to be suspect, but his
prints will never be found here in the no access area, because the kind
of prints he left are not the traceable sort, and it will probably be
weeks before this man reaches into his pocket to discover it is as empty
as any ever has been.

10.
She has no ears but can hear
She has no eyes but can see
She has no nose but can smell
She has no tongue but can taste
She has no fingers
She has no fingers
She has no finger but can touch

11.
She has teeth.
Remember that,
she has teeth.

12.
She has no ears but can hear
his rattle and she knows it
has come from the breeding pen
he can afford only by working those
sixteen hour shifts securing pieces
on radiators gliding ceaselessly
across a conveyer belt ensuring
General Motors will continue
to careen coolly across this continent.

13.

She has no eyes but can see
the purple half moons marking
time on the sky
of his broad dark cheeks
growing more full as he puts in
the extra hours so he can be
available for necessary time
away which is not addressed
on the Western Calendar,
not complaining that his days
consist of eating, sleeping,
driving, and securing
pieces on radiators
gliding ceaselessly through
Midwinter Ceremony
Maple Ceremony
Thunder Ceremony
Planting Ceremony
Strawberry Ceremony
Sun Ceremony
Moon Ceremony
Green Bean Ceremony
Green Corn Ceremony
Harvest Ceremony
Little Water Ceremony
and that because he has worked long enough
he can walk away for the time needed from
that conveyer belt ensuring General
Motors will continue to careen
coolly across this continent.

14.
She has no nose but can smell—
through the layers of crust,
rock, clay, mineral fuels
vast secret reserves
of ore and dirt
resting in the scarred landscape
of his fingers where securing
pieces on radiators gliding
ceaselessly slices new prints unique
to him creating furrows where life thrives
secretly growing in microscopic dances
until strong enough to emerge—
tobacco, tobacco, tobacco he has
burned offering thanks for the sixteen hour
shifts so he can mark the necessary
time which is not
addressed on the Western
Calendar grown vestigial.

15.
She has no tongue but can taste:
the gleaming refined perfect metal
teeth against perfect ancient
teeth as the night
watchman who has all
the keys unzips his uniform
pants and induces friction
sparks in the darkened museum
back room rubbing
his flaccid penis;
the ejaculate he allows
bitter and thick to dry
on her hard palate

slowing and ceasing
the life that thrives secretly, growing
in microscopic dances until strong
enough to emerge, grown so
accustomed, living out entire
complicated spans never seeing
the sun; the victory or vengeance
she has waited five hundred years
for—willing back long enough to take
care of business, lips, soft tissue,
a tongue to shout, shout, shout,
through glass and exhibits where nothing
moves, and will not move, across the state
where he, sleeping off sixteen hour shifts, awakens.

16.
She has no fingers but can touch
that thing inside of him in the middle
of the night, where the purple half moons
careen coolly across the sky
of his broad dark cheeks, that thing
which drives him across this continent
when he is not putting in sixteen hour shifts marking
necessary time not addressed to cast that
digital net hammering the scarred
landscape of his
fingers across all the keys, dropping between
letters igniting microscopic dances in circuitry
of tobacco he has burned
offering thanks for never growing
too tired to look at everything
behind a glass screen, searching for seven generations
of memories and culture and stories born without foot
notes or references to previous footnotes.

She has no fingers but can touch
the transmit key through him,
the breeding pen he can afford only
buying snapping turtles over the internet
casting searches wherever they lead him
finding them in the barren lands of Arizona
where they must proliferate on the surface
plucked like irritable vegetables and shipped
coolly across the span of this continent.

She has no fingers but can touch
the rough shells as they shift sixteen hours
ceaselessly in hostility occasionally careening into one
another where they refuse her condolences
or the tobacco he has burned offering
for their arrivals in the breeding
pen he can afford thanks
where they burrow deep
but never deep enough to reach
the layers of crust, rock, clay
mineral fuels vast secret reserves
of ore or deep enough to disturb the rest
of the giant turtle beneath
where his mother notices their suffering
in the heat and the way they desperately try
to avoid being plucked again and tells him
a story of her grandfather
who had died three years before
he was born, but who was
Christian and therefore his bones were
allowed to turn from memory, flesh, satin,
to ash, dust, stone, crust, rock, clay
mineral fuels igniting a soul in the darkness
no human alive has seen, and he would object

to his place in the chain of seven generations of memories
and culture and stories but he can not halt the accuracy
of his life no book can match.

17.
In his field the year before he died it sat one late summer evening
announcing he was done for the night, at first the old man mistaking
the snapper for a rock somehow unearthed in his last sweep worrying he
was maybe not fit for the plow anymore, relieved when the rock sprang to
life and nicked him, and he remembered they have teeth, this ancient
cracked shell beast teaching lessons even in its old age, scaly leather
against his own shaking brittle and thorny hands laughing as he bled and
moved, even in his seventies, faster than that creature, jerking
furiously in his withering arms, dropping it in a porcelain enameled
basin, with grass, water, and the belief that curious mice would wander
through the drainage hole resting against the dark earth, and everyone
could hear it long into the night spinning itself against the white
prison gleaming blue in the moonlight trying to push its way through the
hole back to the layers and maybe trying to awaken its giant relative
having slept so long that her grandfather had forgotten it entirely, as
he had this one he had intended to release back into the swamp but
planting time came and by the time he remembered the snapper, it had
expired and he threw its skeletal remains in the woods where it slowly
worked its way back into the earth not a half mile from the swamp from
which it had the misfortune of being displaced.

18.
Those old ones, he tells her, they don't make
for decent rattles, too thick, cracked, as he removes
himself for another sixteen hours leaving her
to watch his snappers shift ceaselessly
in hostility occasionally careening
into one another burrowing back.

19.
She tries to water them, his
mother hoping to grow
their survival just this once praying
these irritable vegetables would root
themselves, spread their anger like weeds across
this continent reclaiming its surface
vast secret reserves a blanket
of ceaselessly hostile shifting
shells, unable to stand
their suffering, and he
wonders after her
complaint that he is cruel
but she is
Catholic now and must understand the acute nature
of suffering, and this is what he does.

20.
He seizes one when he has needs
plucking below the surface before
it knows tobacco will be
burned offering thanks for
the accurate grip between two
fingers keeping the cranium cradling
memories and culture and stories from
burrowing deeper into its shell of
thirteen purple moons careening coolly
into one another across the broad
sky of its back, disconnecting
the consecutive links of spinal column
with a quiet twist the only combination
he has been given, blood
pouring out songs between
teeth he has remembered

in each drop hitting the dry earth
new kernels grow another
seven generations as he relieves
the shell of its burden burying
the bones turning from flesh
to memory, from ash
to satin, from dust to stone boiling
from the cranium an accuracy
no book can match to that place
she can touch in the space
he has burrowed, living out
an entire span never seeing
the sun and in the vast secret
reserves they start by sacrificing
the turtle leaving only the hole
of its desperate journey a landmark
that will fill in with his mother's
next watering, in bleaching even
the smallest crevices mapping the broad
cranium granting the turtle another
shot at immortality, refilling
the empty shell planting songs
of dried kernels, songs he has heard
asleep the purple half moons fading
from the sky of his, songs he can
not understand but can
sing just the same, songs another
mother has taught him, songs Indigenous
Woman, Probably Onondaga learned
in the space between her
world and this one, learned
as the giant turtle gave
up rooting below
her when she needed

a place beneath mythical
or not to live and now
needs and has found
ways of producing
a trail she can follow home, songs

21.
of flight songs
of flight beyond songs
of flight beyond Skywoman songs
of flight beyond Skywoman and songs
of flight beyond Skywoman and her songs
of flight beyond Skywoman and her survival.

22.
He burns offering thanks tobacco before
the nonsmoking flight which takes him
closer to Skywoman and her survival
before bringing him to the Museum where
there exists a back room to which he has not
the combination, and he wanders the halls past
a night watchman clearly not on
duty smiling an unlikable smile, rattling
a song using all the keys
in his pocket, unaware he is passing
on the words necessary for that
moment willing back long enough
to take care of five hundred years
worth of business lips, soft tissue,
tongue of Indigenous Skywoman, Probably
Onondaga who sings for her great great great
grandson in the hall giving him
the song his mother

does not
know, can never know
and he hears the words in the teeth
of those keys and he hears her
fingers there rubbing
the flaccid penis behind polyester
and he pulls from his own
pocket the turtle shaking it back
and forth matching her song before
gliding coolly across the continent
on the redeye safely landing again
on the back of the giant
sleeping turtle resting while
he resumes his sixteen hour shifts securing
pieces for her to arrive home
finding the earth stripped
from the smallest crevices mapping
seven generations of memories and
culture and stories born of bones,
bones, bones, filling in with the song he can
not translate the song turning from
stone, dust, and ash to
satin, flesh, memory, the song:

23.
She has teeth
remember
that she has teeth.

24.
This is what he does.

the green corn moon

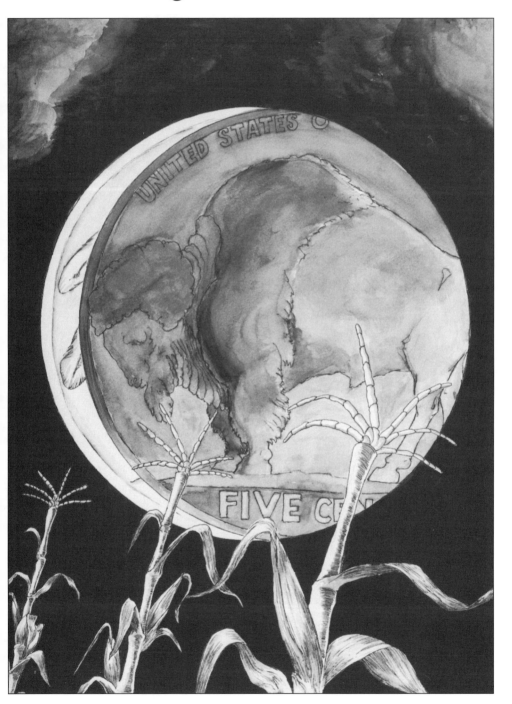

Father and Sun

As the sun left us
in the field
that day
amid the hay
so recently forced
and lashed into unnatural
angular shapes
we laughed and sweated
our way
building on a
wagon foundation
precarious
miniature cities
of bales.

Later in
final light
sweat dry
on my bare chest
and his streaked and
stretched T-shirt
long shadows follow him
and his tractor
as I do
perched on the wagon
amid the fragile
hay cities.

He glances back
and takes my picture
with an invisible camera

maintaining
for posterity
the relationship
neither of us
knows naturally.

And this is safe
to admit amid
the cooling shadows
of August
as the hay metropolis
will soon be dismantled
feed for his cows
and the camera's film
is held silently
protected within our eyes.

Transportation

I didn't stop when I saw
her tonight twenty-four hours
later outlined in the same
streetlamp illumination
this fall night still
wrapped in the stain
covered hooded sweatshirt
beneath a too large broken
zippered leather jacket

this woman I had offered
help, breaking my
hitchhiking rule believing
she was a desperate teenager,
having been there, myself, trying
to catch rides off the reservation,
holding out my dark thumb dutifully
ignored once I left the boundaries
of home, when I pulled onto the cindered
shoulder last night, my caution
lights turning her transiently red
as she ran toward my heated car

only to discover
in the gauge light
her cracked lips
pulled hard over
what few teeth she
spoke her lies through
even those blackening
in the earnest epic she told
others, attempting

to believe it, herself.
I wondered who tonight
would hear about her car
having just broken
down as she headed
out to get milk
for her kids' Lucky Charms
while she directed her
Samaritan to the outdoor
all night streetside markets
where the white substance
is sold in small
distilled rocks
not cartons.

Late August Sunsets

The dark spots grow rapidly
spreading across our lawns
and lives so neatly tended
banishing color
pushing the wild
edge closer
enveloping us.

I lift the heavy
camera and focus
trying to catch her
one last time
in the remaining
light but she moves
and faces the darkness.

As she turns away
the deep brown wells
of her drawn face
that had moments before
been eyes, cheeks, smile
flood the areas
where her skull does not reside.

"Put that thing
away. You're just like
those damn hospital
people, always taking
pictures, taking pictures,"
she says, from the hungry shadows
and coughs.

Night Music

Years ago we sat and watched overhead
among the soot and sirens of city
existence Canada Geese who mate, but
do not flock, for life appear
unexpectedly emerging from the dark
sharp early fall air, their bellies
glowing orange in unnatural
industrial light from factories
blocks away ambitious night fliers
wings cutting ammonia tainted
atmosphere, their voices acknowledging
time together dissonant
counterpoint to the factory time clocks.

Under another patch of sky less orange
with chemicals, we take momentary
comfort in pretending the overhead March
flappers in the eastern sky
announcing their arrival
as they glide low and push echoes
across the water are just
this once the same
ones we have seen for years,
and we sit still together
watching and knowing this
momentary lie is not necessary and
that this shared vision is the only
constant we need.

A Few Good Jokes

That this city never sleeps is a lie, or at least a half truth
this night in September closing at twelve
when the fountain rests and the floods burn slowly
from white to red, their electronic arcs winking out
our long shadows bleeding forward, obscuring all
where minutes before anonymous groups passed
us walking among the monoliths where you swept your vibrant hands
presenting the blunt grace of Chagall paintings hanging in the Met
and I pretended I recognized style
as well as I had name, trying to fill the reservation
cavity of my memory with a worldliness I will never achieve
regardless of the number of exhibit catalogues
I can buy or Arts Council panels I serve on forever
the rube from upstate who nodded and smiled well enough.

The vast time you have spent here deepens my ignorance, passions
exploding even now, ghosts in your ears as you celebrate the music
which drives you in divergent directions, that first I can see in
your eyes, hear within your voice as you describe symphonies I can not
hear, and I grow more faint in the fading light, consumed
by the knowledge of these passions, and the abilities you have to walk
away from fires that insistent, that in your youth, you drove hours
along dark mountain roads to learn from a master, an instrument you
would eventually abandon in a dismissal of near greatness, that
the only time you would pick it up again after having set aside
the clarinet would be to show your daughter the proper fingering
techniques, as she gently lighted her own fires, prodded from the
embers of your talent and drive, and I know I am less than a keystroke
away at any moment from disappearing entirely.

Drawn to your promise on a computer chat service, I depressed
the enter button and sent a greeting, asking after those few
good jokes of yours and we fell quietly, as has happened only rarely
in my life, into natural, easy conversation, occasionally laughing
out loud to an empty room in rattling keys unlocking that elusive
something between friends between words, letters, comfort
and companionship turning ourselves blue in the glow of cathode ray
letters shooting themselves across a monitor screen into hot August
nights where, drawn by forces they can not grasp, small insects waste
their short lives wandering the perimeter, trying to penetrate the
glass screen, hoping to find the source of that blue fire, knowing
its heat will be even worth dying for and by the time you left into
the void of disconnection that first night, my desk was littered
with the still bodies of those who never gave up their quest.

Over time, we agree to meet on my next trip into the city and you give
me instructions on where this will occur, and I pretend to know
the location of Avery Fisher Hall, confident I will find it,
in my new cosmopolitan self, and am reminded of my origins only
moments after arriving at the Lincoln Center complex wondering why you
had called a gazing pool a "fountain" to discover shortly I was not
even remotely where I thought I was, the fountain nearly half a block
from my snide location at the time, a fact I do not disclose when we
finally do connect an hour or so later, keeping my stupidity to myself
even over dinner at Fiorello's across Broadway where from our sidewalk
table, the fountain is still visible, but not the pool, discreetly
obscured behind the building I now know the name of and will forever,
being gazed upon by others more aware of their surroundings than I and
by dessert the edge of my inexperience has dulled some.

Later, we pass through Central Park, and I am drunk on a freedom
I have never imagined could exist, dismissing the shadows Olmstead
never intended as hiding places for all the dangers a city could
conjure, experiencing the place as it should be, emerging confident
from the south gate, that I could even live in this place, spend any
night defying muggers and anything else festering just below the
level of awareness around me, eyeing sympathetically a man on the
bench across from us, clearly organizing his entire life's belongings
into a dirt-streaked back pack, forgetting a life so easily
compressible was one I had carried on my back for years, and in my new
height, I allow myself the luxury of eye contact, knowing he will see
our mutual history, but the back pack man engages me in conversation
just long enough to tell me a stupid joke, then demands money for his
cleverness and only your assertiveness keeps him from collecting.

Crossing at that shining globe near the south entrance, we look up
and glimpse those places which have been our homes, and I try to
describe frybread to you: the taste, as butter runs from it down
your chin, at the National Picnic, where the frybread cook, arms
grease scarred from years of living this role, shouts out the same
thing he says every summer at this time, about how he knows he has
kneaded the dough enough when all the dirt is gone from under his
fingernails, and even though you secretly believe he is really only
half joking, you don't care because you have carefully coordinated
your bites to run out of frybread as you soak up the last smoky drops
from a cornsoup bowl's bottom while the sun goes down and the
fireball is ignited for this year's game, and some will wear their
new scars wide, but I fail to convey this in the same way you can not
make me see oceanlike tobacco fields miles long from your old home.

These blank spaces fill my head with a demanding void as I can not
picture even what a tobacco plant looks like, can not see those
mountain roads of your youth, headlights seeking out each dangerous
cliff begging to be driven over and no matter how I try to describe
the taste and look and feel of Indian corn, I know the only way to
truly accomplish this is to take you there and walk those roads, sit
at the picnic grove, to find the beauty in this life, to see that
while not Chagall or Bach there is a signature in an old woman's
hands' grind of the dried corn kernels from a braid, raining it down
into an enameled kettle, music, but your silence at my mention of the
reservation tells me, as we cross traffic, go against masses leaving,
dodge cabs, arrive at this riotous fountain where the evening began
hours ago, we will only ever meet in this neutral place, neither yours
nor mine, our friendship in that distant, abstract place it began.

We stand long under the last remaining light beneath the concrete
awning at the entrance to the parking garage where I am reluctant
to let this night end regardless of what the City of New York
thinks, and you offer to hail me a cab, or at least to show me
how, as if I have never done this before, so you will be the one left
standing on the darkened concrete, knowing the dangers of anonymous
shadows like I have somehow never learned to see beyond the simple
roads where I have walked my whole life, as if they were not as
dangerous because I knew the people who hid in the dark looking for
opportune moments, and as we embrace, our shadows merging, I know
I can not halt time and absorb what I can, scent, sensation, those
hands, and letting go, slowly, watch you descend the stairs to
the spot where your family sedan waits and I do not move
until you have turned the corner into muted obscurity.

I sit on the darkened steps, feeling the chill of autumn
permeating denim in a way I am sure the trees in Central Park
know it is September and they, like us, are waiting for the first
to turn and drop, obscuring the path with their wake
not meeting the expectant gaze of cab drivers desperate
to take me to my choice of destination
but I do not hail one until I feel your absence
that empty underground parking spot gaping as you pass
through the Lincoln Tunnel, entering New Jersey
and your world beyond where I resume my role
as white letters falling into a black screen churning
out dedications to someone who has long moved beyond
my place and if I close my eyes here I can almost see
the tail lights fade in the darkness of the future.

the fresh moon

The Annoyance of Evolution

The connection reasserted itself
through the unsuspecting cord
of my office extension
from the woman who hadn't called
herself your wife since before
I was born.

Dad's under the knife tonight
she said, the same way she might have
told me she was out of bread:
that faint, unspoken suggestion
that I should do something
to alter the inconvenient physics
of the moment, as if I could
perform miracles by pure thought
sending endless loaves
as monuments to my prosperity
through the phone lines
to her table,
or pretending I had ever called
you by that name.

I had fully expected,
traveling unfamiliar roads
wondering why you had chosen
a hospital so far from your home
to engage in emergency surgery,
that it had to be on your liver.

As I rode the elevator
with the others

they told me it was your appendix
a useless reminder of a former life
enflamed and nagging—
could happen to anyone.

You came out all right
and to make conversation
in the unfamiliar room
having thirty years of nothing
to say, I asked why
you had picked this place
miles and miles away, and you said
that everyone knows you hate
the one at home and
they nodded with you
at me in my ignorance.

On Meeting My Father in a Bar for the First Time

I am about
eighteen
when I step through
that door and hide
myself in the room
lit only with red bulbs
disappearing into
the darkened, bitter
room full of red-faced friends
or maybe just acquaintances
who grow close
and become friends
when their pockets fill
with beer sweat and nothing.

Sidling up to some
potentials, I nod
and smile that smile
which will buy me
at least a draft
at last call
just before the white lights
come up and I am
the only one
in the place
left with red skin.

My first swallow
half foam
is interrupted
by a shoulder tap from

a previous potential
who knows where I come from
pointing and asking me
if that guy is anything
to me.

I shake my head
sipping and laughing
and turn my back
on the form I had stepped over
passed out in the doorway
reeking of piss and betrayal.

Toronto, More or Less, in Fifteen Years

1.
"Hey! This place? That's
an Indian word, Means
the 'place of meeting'.
Right? You've heard that
before, right?"

2.
I am told or asked that at some
point every time I am
in this place, and though
I have heard that is
a literal translation of a Huron
word, I can neither
confirm nor deny this, not being
or knowing Huron, and if they know
this already, why are they
asking me? Do they think we are
going to spontaneously talk Huron
to one another once they convince
me they can? That we will have something
in common now, more than just this "place
of meeting?"

3.
All my life, those towers rose
vaguely across the water, that life
growing in my imagination like a tree
whose roots withstood rot below
the surface, while I consumed cheap domestic
lakeside beer at sunset watching those monuments

darken against the scorching sky as the buzz
set in before we had to make our way back home
where that city was exotic streets, restaurants,
a mall housing sculpted Canada geese, forever
frozen in mid-flight swooping through a glass
corridor, filtered through static and snow
imprisoned in a second-hand television where we would watch
even the French speaking station, understanding
nothing, long into the night, marveling at a place
so wild they broadcast signals while most people slept.

4.
The first time I am
nineteen, and not
driving, still get lost
in the simple grid
of my home town's streets.
You have brought me
here and we spend
hours one day looking
for a park that does
not exist, because I had
read about it once.
I lose to the pressure for days
the hearing in my right ear,
but the sights from the tower
my home, that spot I have spent
so many years dreaming from, microscopic
on the horizon the reservation
smaller than my eyes
can afford, perspective
worth the cost.

5.
Diminished in one
year, but only in
forbidding heights, this city seems
like home when we arrive
after a month on the road
sleeping in the best hotels'
parking garages, shoving
money through stainless steel
slots at bullet proof L. A.
gas stations, flying
for the first time ever
through the Grand
Canyon too dumb and naïve
to recognize a rough
flight, mistaking the sharp
odor of the pilot's fear
for sweat as he keeps
both hands on the controls, pointing
with his stubbled chin
to the contrasting specks on the chasm
floor, explaining they are the homes
of a tribe living within
the rocky confines, entire lives
spent in the shadows, and from there having
crossed two countries in four weeks,
I no longer check my pockets
every five minutes to see
if I have been relieved
of my wallet in the shadows grown
pale of these orderly walls.

6.

Elaborating over Scotch whiskey
and some unpronounceable French dish
in a bistro where she has chosen
to take me in an effort to soften
her rejection, she offers this
anecdote, as to why she feels
we simply can not continue:

      "It's not . . .
      the blacks who are
      feared and homeless
      in this city,
      it's the Natives who have
      left the reserve only
      to litter the TTC subway grate
      trying to find warmth."

7.

Along the walls of some anonymous
tower on Queen a tall dark man who cuts
the sun from my path, his long
hair matted and rough pocked skin
pulled tight like a rotting water
drum against his skull gleaming
with grime, asks me for change
and when I offer to buy him
a hot dog from the vendor he repeats
his request, and I give up
every coin in my pocket and keep
walking, knowing if our lives should
ever bisect again his cheeks will be
stretched even further, waiting for that
stick to come down, crack his skull,
stop the beat for good.

8.
Again on Queen, a man in a streaked white
T-shirt hallucinates his way
along the concrete, arguing with his
reflection in the trendy plate
glass windows of shops I had successfully
ignored randomly strikes a woman walking in
the opposite direction
and as I try to console her while others
catch the man, she keeps repeating
the red skin on her cheek throbbing
her voice thick with British
accent, "I never expected it
from him, or I would have crossed over."

9.
Up on Church one November night at a stop
light a young woman wanders awkward
up to my passenger's side window
the gooseflesh on her bare thighs
making her more reptilian than
the spiked leather boots which end just above
her knees and keep her constantly off
balance in the rain, and though she knows
from one glance that I am equally reservation
exotic in this city, canceling out her one
advantage over the others who think I am looking
for some company by the hour and the act, she stays
a minute to enjoy the company of one who knows
what it is like to walk dark roads and look up
expecting nothing more than the stars and the moon
or maybe it is just to feel the heat of my vents
on her face until the light changes, and we are
no longer red together, as she steps back and I
pull off into the night.

10.
Those boys—rez accents
still dense in their throats
reflecting off canyons of polished
glass where we see each other
first, a few years
younger and a few dollars shorter
than I am at the time—spot
sympathy in my braid lying
heavily across my back, five
years of patience marked in
its weave, and ask for some
help with their dream.
"Parris Island," they say
"That's where we want
to be, Marines, man, Marines."
They tell me they want to sell
their hair to finance their journey
knowing a place, they tell me, that pays
a hundred a foot, and they grasp handfuls
of commodity from their skulls, shake it
loose, and claim a grand, easy
between them, but the place only buys it
already cut, and they need just a few
bucks to hire a blade, and could I spare
it, I wasn't getting a haircut anytime
soon they observed. As always, I gave
it up, not bothering to point out where
they have come from will forever keep them
out of the Marines, that they should come up
with a better story than that, but the stories
they tell are no good at home anyway so maybe
they are better off here, selling
their lives by the inch.

11.

Hot dog carts line the sidewalk outside
of the Eaton's Center, where the Canada
geese still remain static, never reaching
their migratory destination, collecting
dust in the air above me, nearly forgotten
as reality builds its own nest, fragments
from other places, in my cranium, well
dressed people before me making dual
purchases, feeding torn bits
of flesh to the pigeons who have
made this corner their home, laughing
as the birds rip and fight over the meat, pushing
closer for one more piece, being rewarded
by these people who complain to each other
after an Elder reduced to role of Old
Woman loses the intimidation game to a more savvy
pigeon with a sharper eye that there truly are people
who do not belong in this place (of meeting).

12.

In the second level below
ground at the Eaton's
where Queen and Yonge converge, in the First
Nations Gift shop, I run into, nearly collide
with Haduii, falseface masks so far
removed from Longhouses, and
ceremonies they belong to, hanging
in rows like lynched men, their long
hair tangling in one another's, crooked
mouths grimacing and metal eyes glowing
blankly, oblivious to the tags dangling
from their sides, like cardboard earrings
whispering disclaimers that they are

decoration only, not meant for ceremonial
usage, yet they must be deaf, and beg me
for tobacco anyway, but I have given up
smoking ten years before.

13.
Back on the street, at sea level again, I
still see their hair
is real, coarse and black, whispered
in the mask tags' fine print
below the five hundred
dollar price code, that minute line
informing me these masks were hand made
by Indigenous people from the natural fibers
    of rez boys wanting to be U.S. Marines,
    of rez men floating further away on subway updrafts
    of rez women who have become mothers to the Pigeon Clan
    of rez girls whose moccasins are patent leather with spikes
and I descend again to take them all home, and they laugh
as I attempt to lift them from their hooks, stopping
realizing theirs are not the only gleaming
eyes in the room, that humming
echo of the surveillance camera following
me as I enter the elevator and the way out emptyhanded.

14.
Back on the U.S. shore
of Lake Ontario, in Autumn, gourmet coffee
replacing that sunset beer for
fear of a DWI, somehow having
been infused with respectability

a Mohawk friend and I watch the shafts of this
city's skyline rise up and darken from the lake's
edge as they do each day at this time, and she
mentions a recent article she read suggests the name
is really a variation on a Mohawk word, describing
a place where the trees stand in the water which
seems as good a description as any at this point
and I wait, the air chewing on the ridges
of my ears, for dormancy to enter, and as it does, I
turn, heading home.

15.
"Hey! This place? That's
an Indian word, Means
the 'place of meeting'.
Right? You've heard that
before, right?"

These Nights I Know You Have Struck a Deal with My Mother

Though she had only one rule for me, to get home
before the sun came up or have called the night
before to let her know where I would be finding a place
to sleep, I am sure she drifted only at the moment
I entered the door, drifting myself to my unmade bed
upstairs, trying to not hit the walls too hard,
and while I have learned to take stairs two at a time
on even the best Scotch, the cars and bullets I dodged
years ago fly by me now and again, and I know why
she was relieved if my calls came from a reservation
house no matter whose it was.

It is three in the morning, and I know
how much you hate staying up late, how at midnight
you get that look like: "Aren't you ever going
to go to bed?" if I am writing too long, and here
I am, sitting, listening to old music miles
from the reservation, and hoping the phone
does not ring thinking I might just let the machine
get it if it does, constructing the statements
in as official words as I can conjure, that the police
are going to deliver: do they say "body" or "corpse,"
I wonder, checking that clock and it is still
three in the morning, maybe three-oh-one.

Home Work

For the first time
I did not push you
to phone the doctor
knowing the answer
was yes this instance
and after that
initial consultation
I waited for that call
like I had no other
having emptied waste
baskets where blood
made its presence known
smeared across tissue
you had buried
in the bottom hoping
I would find it I suspect
as earlier, it refused
to leave facecloths and towels
you washed in solitude
while I worked
trying to hide
the wildly dividing
cells asserting themselves
on your skin.

the harvest moon

Sirens

I.
They say sirens call men
to their deaths
and the only part
I might argue with
is at home
women (having equal
standing as men)
are not
left out.

II.
Sirens like newborns
come screaming into the night
as we doze
allowing ourselves only
the sleep of contempt.

While the comfort
of flame calls
sweetly, we wait
never to be caught
unaware of those lures
gleaming and dancing
like jewels only
until the wood runs out
and we're left
with empty frostbitten hands.

III.
We sat in summer evening shrouds
as years and deaths
squawked into our lives
on hard benches
doing penance
for listening
to a chorus
of sirens
          (humming through our back woods)
and Cobra police scanners
poised to spit
off-key harmonies
of recognizable names
into our own controlled
bonfire flames where
by alchemy and determination
we turned failures
to ashes.

IV.
Laying in bed late
when firetrucks sing
oppressively overriding
radio talkshow host who
between jingles for the Supermarket
Liquors Columbus Day sale
on Thunderbird fortified wine
and Crazy Horse Malt Liquor
discusses the high mortality rate
among young minorities
I hear statistics for

African Americans,
Latin Americans,
Asian Americans,
Haitian Americans,
Cuban Americans,
Near Eastern Americans,
Far Eastern Americans,
Indian Americans,
I assume
to regain sleep
that the American Indians
were drowned out by the now
drifting siren trying
to believe it is too far
for a reservation call.

V.
I am bathed in a film
of night grease and red light
as fire trucks pull in
and I greet my unexpected guests
in their rubber coats:

Don, who lost his fortune when
his fire
        (we're all required to have
        at least one per lifetime,
        more if you're lucky)
turned the contents of
his (not so)strong box
into dollar dust
and a sludgy pile of silver and copper
a swirled marble cake at a
Burn-Victim Benefit Dinner,

smiles as he tugs on the hose
alcohol thick breath pluming out daring
January night air to
freeze his life

Billy, who still wears the hard-
on he carried all day for his wife
       (he tells over intimate beers
        in the volunteer firefighters' bar)
some duties are more urgent
than others he says
pulling out and
pulling on some jeans
wouldn't you want someone
to do it for us he asks her
as the siren calls his name,
finds when the fire is out
in my garage a dead Thunderbird
bottle and an empty pack of Camels.

Joe, whose wife didn't care
if he had a hard-on or not and
threw him out and
who was not
there suddenly days later
is ponytailless, a dark burn
in a sunless season
riding his neck instead and
he has quit drinking and
smoking, but still smolders
I think.

VI.
When Violet's sirens were heard
on the reservation
I had lived

in the city for
five years or more.

Her years of contributions at the volunteer firefighter
and ambulance corps bingo did not save her
their Jaws of Life Machine
would be purchased in the Fall.
Many who heard had already been
waiting for the song
to begin.
The other car that greeted hers
at ninety miles an hour
dragged her freshly empty
of children (safely deposited at Sunday school) stationwagon
across the reservation border
loud enough for most to flip
on their scanners and wait.

Even if the urban air
could have carried the song,
I would not have heard it.
I stopped hearing
those city sirens
after the first year,
when I could finally
convince myself I did not know
the person being called.

But my cousin Sheryl
at a city estate sale
shopping for some
dead man's clothes
that might fit her husband
          (somehow knowing he
          less than three years
          later would need a suit
          having heard his own

sirens tuning up late one Sunday
down on Ridge Road)
sang Violet's siren song
for me not even an hour
after the fact.

VII.

Telinda's sirens
I did hear.
To celebrate my new
job and recognition
off the reservation
I came back to it
bearing gifts.

My family and I
cracked the seal
on some Absolut Vodka
around my sister's dining room
table we were not fooling around
when we heard it
they first
I having lost
that radar poured
another round until
the singers were less than half
a mile away.

We stood at the road's edge
where Telinda wrapped her car
like a gift
around a telephone pole
in an attempt to slow down
the news of her death
which set off a reaction

in my fellow siren seekers
Mark, Matt, Dawn
who went on a three day binge
          (one day for each)
even risking law
as well as death
in greasy alcohol-red skin
trying to find me
in the city.

I was not
there but home
watching the bonfire jewels fly
and listening for sirens
that would tell me
my friends had found
the telephone pole
they were always looking for.

Mystic Powers (I)

I imagine my mother
hates the mystical powers
she's been saddled with
plodding through our futures
in damp tea leaves
chipped cups and spit
regretting the worst fortune
she ever told me:
that by the time
I discovered I didn't belong
in the white world
it would be too late
to come home.

She could not see
clearly in the bottom
of my cracked and mended tea cup
the fragments delivering
after their fashion
my fractured future.
Passing the cup
she tried to show me
where the leaves said I was
fading but I saw only dregs
and she said "See,"
as if trying to will my vision back
"it has started already."

She watched me every year
wondering how it would play out
if I would be shot or stabbed
or catch some incurable disease
among the crazy white people
while I grew by the year
more and more pale
even as I learned to braid
and tame my wild hair
a tenuous cord never
quite long enough to
reach the family plot she shared
with fifty or so cousins.

As always, she was right.
By the time I was ready
to walk reservation roads again
I no longer had a destination there.
Not having bothered to read
her own fortune for years,
knowing better than to think
she even had one,
my mother had not seen
the house fire
which had wiped us clean
from the map
the year before.

Wine and Cheese

Mike and me
two reservation boys
in a plush, carpeted living room
(some friend of his from school)
need to be told
to use the coasters
(having thought they were
small decorative petrified
wood pieces)
when placing the crystal
long-stemmed wine goblets
on the glass-top coffee table.

We stare longingly
at the lonely block
of pale cheese which is difficult
to see on the almost
matching tea-party plate set
before us
so different
from the heavy orange
bricks that have our families'
work-dirty fingerprints and
GOVERNMENT SURPLUS—NOT FOR RESALE
adorning their sides.

As we walk the rutted
roads of home later
Mike tells me
he knew there was
more cheese
in that guy's fridge

could see it glowing
through the white
enamel door
but the plate stayed
empty at least
until we left.

We finished the night
at his mother's kitchen
table with the rest
of his family
eating cheese as long
as the brick lasted
and sipping from wine
glasses by Welch's.

The Dirt on My Hands

As you had the last time
you would probably hate this poem
I have written about you
staying mad for a year
letting me know of your anger through
friends and not listening as I spoke
of your failure to read what was really there
and our friends grew tired of passing
news and began to pretend they knew us
in different universes, the same ones
we used for not running
into each other at the same
powwows where sometimes fewer
than fifty people tried to fill
a room with tradition.

The last time I saw you
we crossed one another
at the supermarket while
I chatted up an old teacher
having moved into that
territory myself, acknowledging
stubborn ignorance and from nowhere
you shifted into that secret
face you always made when you teased
me as you had thousands
of times before those letters
printed on the page, my worries
about your drinking, transformed
themselves into accusations as they rode
down your visual cortex.

That day, we spoke of old
times ignoring that damaged bridge
of years and even laughed over events
we both witnessed from our separate
universes and I walked away, finally,
smiling, believing we would flip to see
who bought cornsoup and frybread at the next
Grand River powwow in July. But Grand
River is next week, and there won't be any
frybread gambling with you this year. The last
time I did see you was when they closed the casket
of your own making this afternoon, and I grabbed that clot
of earth with the others and let it rain down
on the lid as they lowered you and, wondering what
my share in all of this was, I picked up another handful.

Fall Leaves

Dust from my sister's car suspends the setting
sunlight in the air sharpening its tongue before
us, and my niece waves with a ferocity so strong
she makes the dust spin in miniature whirlwinds until
she feels herself grow small enough to hide
behind one of those grains resting on the filmed glass
of the rearview mirror.
She neatly rips open the foil sleeve wrapping the gift
her father presented her just before departing for being
good, for not crying two consecutive weeks as they started
the autumn bowling season, starting the yearly cycle of
Saturday nights with her uncle—the gift, a candy bar divided
neatly into twin segments, one for each dry eye, he told
her as he started the car.

She offers one to me and I take it, unable to assert
the better judgement I am paid to have, as her fifty cents
an hour babysitter, and watching it vanish so quickly, she offers
the second, and lets the wrapper disappear among the dead
leaves surrounding us, as I take it and pray for dust to settle
and shroud the crumbs on my hands.

Your Garden

It is a wonder,
you did not grow
tired planting seed after
seed only to see
them not germinate
fall to rot, slugs and worms
in soil not ready or willing
enough to be receptive:

those sophisticated beds of notes
in combination and orchestration
at the hands of masters dissolved
and ground down in favor of three
chord power pop, music in its most
simple and uninteresting forms, thick
weeds of bombastic progression;

a trench coat and blazer
cultivated and woven perfect left to
turn fallow behind the dandelion brashness
of callused cowhide, scraped until it
gleamed with drama the animal
world never intended, adorned with metal
in case the leather itself did not draw
enough attention.

But, that day you opened
the door to Talking Leaves Book
Sellers on Main Street in Buffalo—
that city itself a remote and exotic
impression on my reservation
mind—you tilled my brain

so fresh that gulls swooped
in to examine the furrows
for what might be lurking
in that dense mess
at that point so overgrown
with Stephen King and nothing
else, that the birds rose all
noise and fury at the emptiness
while you stood, and sweated
as only you have been willing
to do, ignoring the dark circles
of strain this causes you,
planting words I had
never even imagined.

Books, real books
in neat lines, so many
I nearly froze among
the orderly rows not knowing
which way I should turn
to face this new found sun
burning all around me, but again
there you walked, moving purposefully
over titles and names, letters
strung together on spines, picking
them from their places among
the others and smiling, moved on
your harvest a feast set before
my starving eyes.

Stranger in a Strange Land
More Than Human

Support, pollination, fiction
beyond the real but grounded

solid, allowing for that new
direction, spreading farther
than the bounds of my experience.

Were you relieved when after waiting
and waiting for what must have seemed
like endless drought years, those first
letters sprouted from my fingertips
tentative, misshapen, poorly
formed but there, just the same?

Being the expert gardener you are
you gently pinched off gangly
sentences begging to be trimmed
and pruned, tied dangling participles
neatly back, provided nourishment
and attention, and waited even longer
than any gardener should have a mind to
and I have to wonder, after all this time,
as I sit here now, and you are exploring another
uncultivated garden, if you have found this
field all worthwhile,
your sunset harvest.

the hunting moon

Birthday Wishes

She turns sixty-nine
again
this year afraid

She won't
      cook dinner
      do laundry
      give rides
            and dollars
            and advice
            and time
            and blood
            and life

            And those receiving
her gifts quietly hide
that
landmark
candle

denying the flame
or the chance
to snuff it
out

on that top shelf
where she could
not reach,
if she
wanted.

Black Leather Jacket

You dangled unaware
on your hook
as I remembered
her mentioning you
quietly one night
over her gritty coffee,
your anticipated
embrace the end
to my sore-footed search
one arm
casually tucked
into a front pocket
maybe reaching for smokes
or perhaps ready to reveal
a brilliant set of keys,
saying "It's about time."

December twenty-third brought
me to you
the question mark carved
into my greasy brow
a little different
from those other
pleading faces
desperately conjuring
lingerie sizes
from minds that have
forgotten the last time
they said "I love you,"
to the women in their lives
and really meant it.

As I bathed in household
appliances she'd never have
the inclination to learn
knowing she preferred over any
food processor the scarred
paring knife which has tasted
pints of her blood by now,
I could hear her already:
"You lose touch
if you don't feel the work."

If I dragged running
water, a commode, a septic system
to her home, slipping them in
through one of the gaping holes
where the wreck refused
to continue masquerading
as a house
would she turn her back
wash herself clean
of my city influence
and throw me out the back door
with her dirty water?

Her dignity was beyond my
meager success, anyway
but the $129.99 price
tag before me was not.
Your sultry, gleaming
skin called to me.
I longed to trace
the floral growth
etched into your tasteful
patches of rough skin,
resembling the rose bushes

she had grown
when she'd had the time
to keep the thorns from taking over.
"Roses don't put food
on the table," she'd said
when, at twelve, I asked
about her robust thorn bushes.
"Mrs. DeBartellomeo gives
twenty-five a day, just for a once a week cleaning,
Twenty-five.
No rose bush
is gonna give that kind
of wage," she said
chasing me out the door
so she could cook
for her brother
for my brothers
and sisters
and me
in peace.

I presented you to her
Christmas morning
and she rubbed your skin
following the same patterns
I had at the store,
trying you on
and snatching glances
of you and her together
in the mirror
before telling me
to return you.

As I drove you back
to the store defeated
I heard her voice instead
of the quad sound system
in my fast car.
"I wouldn't recognize myself,"
she said.
"And besides, where
would I wear it?
Emptying the pot?
Burning the garbage?
Save your money.
Save your money.
Save your money."

Traditional Blanket

She wraps herself in
the comforting itch
of a reservation
blanket she has worn
so long it holds her
shape even
in those rare moments
she steps
tentatively from
its nagging fibers.

It is . . .
the blue one
she tacked to the arch
every winter dividing
her house along
the invisible line where
her father died
leaving her relying on
the state in a home only half
insulated, a synthetic membrane
wheezing in the January winds.

It is . . .
the red one
she saves in the hall
closet to seal those men
in their own rank
hangover juices
on the couch or floor

so she will not see blood
stains, trails of where
they have fallen
every Saturday night.

It is . . .
the white one
of the fabled U.S. Army small
pox shrouds we've all
heard were delivered to
our ancestors
the sort they don't need
to bother with anymore—
we take care
of our own
these days.

It is none of these.
It is all of these.

The Favorite Recipe Card of Many a Reservation Woman
or
Sunday Brunch, Reservations

It takes all
morning so she rises
silently dancing
her graceful steps
across the sharp
linoleum distance waiting
for the heat to kick
in, rubbing her thinning
hands over a steaming pot
of coffee she will not drink—
her shrinking stomach shouting
its last protests—but its dark
aroma drives
the acrid beer sweat
from the new day's air, and these men,
who've grown in body only,
like it black and strong
burning the dry cracks
from their Budweiser lips.

As later they lumber warm from
wherever she and unconsciousness
found them the night
before still
wearing the blankets she
wrapped them in after
last call, she adds their greasy
Sunday hangover

breakfast bacon
tearing free strips
of her own
life every weekend
to feed these shapes
which mumble before her
disappearing form,
never raising
their shiny faces and
bleeding eyes to see her
fading slowly like coffee steam.

the cold moon

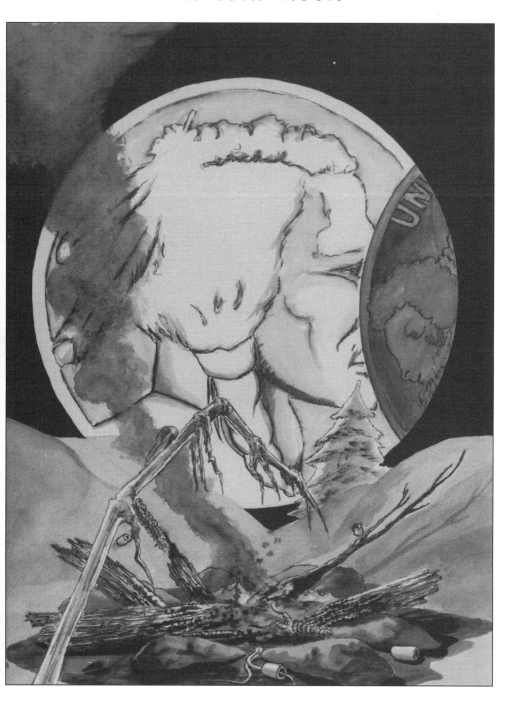

This Last Glass

She'd probably frown
at this last glass
of late night scotch
that I sip sniffing
not its twelve-year-old bouquet
but a vintage more fresh
and demanding
wafting not from my glass
but shouting
from my fingertips.

New soot and fragments
of her life and mine
hang cloying from my extremities
dense gloves of history
through which I have sifted
into the unrelenting darkness
trying to retain
through scorched shirts
and melted photos
fragile moments of our lives.

I think, having trouble
typing these last few lines
my mother would understand
and agree, having herself
succumbed to the dense and forgiving
blanket of Morphine to forget
how she jumped
refusing to let history drag her down
from the burning
home we had shared for two hundred years.

Her Dreams

They involved finding perfection
in a garage sale
furnishing her two-hundred-year-
old house
with others' recycled ideas
till she had gotten it
just right
occasionally mad
when I would not supply
(a victim of inconvenience)
her impetus
with a delivery truck.

They included on occasion
a replacement for the picture
window my niece cracked
gravely with a cueball
on a New Year's Eve
when I had teased her
too much as a child
though I knew she would
never remove the refracted map
which traced our maturity
from spontaneous aggression
to thoughtful wine-tasting.

They melted today
amid the drooling picture window
and haphazard furniture
in the rude flamboyance
of impotent firetrucks

merely lighting and scoring
a symphony of flames
as it performed
without request
encore after encore
before a weeping audience of family
who only wanted the conclusion.

That Old Falseface

It hung for years
on our dining room wall
born of substandard clay
culled for the dull
hands of high school students
its flatline mouth
and empty eyes
the happy face symbol
ironed into neutrality
perhaps suggestive
of my brother's mood
in the art class
where he'd been forced
to make it
having been told
all Indians are artists.

My mother had adopted it
hiding behind it her secrets
suspended by a flimsy nail
and ancient plaster:
the wedding band
she had given up,
the four thousand windfall
she had tried to give us
declaring herself Mrs. Trump
and claiming she had always wanted
better for her children
considering this a fortune
knowing she would never
see a real one,

her plans for a life
she could truly call her own.

We could not find it in the ashes
even its kiln-toughened
features unable to withstand
the relentless housefire
which stole all our hidden dreams
and we were left
with only our own blank
and secretless faces to stare into.

Outgrowing the Zeigler

I lay for years
on the uneven floorboards
defiant nails occasionally piercing
my skin before the kerosene
warmth of my mother's ancient
Zeigler heater, pretending the broken
trademark resembled some television
show icon removing our
primitive heater from the middle
of winter to the hipness
of Hollywood
scaring the rats away, my own
defiance enough for a night of peace.

Winters there
I stretched to
where I could
no longer warm
my growing body before the
Zeigler, twitching and rolling
attempting to make myself
smaller by the year
to ensure my slow bake
was thorough
the rats mad I would not move on
to warmer or more
efficient climates.

Today I watched
as the new propane
heater tanks conspired
with the runaway car
to cook the house
of my childhood
uncontrollably
down to its essence—
home juice—
missing the orphaned kerosene Zeigler
forgotten on the back porch
turned red in its embarrassed
and silent retirement.

Dream House

Every night around three
the house stands again
reassembling itself with some secret
genetic housing code
and, as I pass through the door
climbing the creaking stairs
to our old room
ignoring the fact
that my snapping ankles
sound like the small flames
that refuse to die
rekindling after a fire
is supposedly over,
I wonder in solitude
after my brothers and sisters.

Never do I run
into them staring
out of the room we shared
from old windows, frames
narrow channels littered
with sluggish wasps
unsure of where to strike
their weaving tails,
pane shrouded
in cloudy winter plastic
a cataract obscuring life
beyond the barrier
where we all dreamed awake
of some other existence
beyond the reservation.

At length, I awaken
to the steady repetition
of muted city night sounds
in my well-insulated house
remembering those frames
were among the last
to go, heat shattering the
smoky panes when a fire decided
to take its snapping ankles
for a walk through our history
and I wonder if we concentrated
could my siblings and I reform
our misguided juvenile dreams
support by desperate
support?

Passing Through Breaking Glass

I stand again
at the basswood tree
still able to see
the empty wedge
a smile cut from it
by my mother
who cooked it up
to draw from me years
in the past glass hidden
below the surface changing
my fingerprints forever
at unexpected shifts
the damp wood and shards
gleaming from her
proud hands the proof
that old Indian medicine works
even for boys stupid or angry
enough to punch windows.

Though the scar has
grown as they do
dull, gray with age
mimicking the belligerent
and coarse outer layers,
the nature of survival,
I remember the cut
her old paring knife
splintering bark and
glistening with sap
and feeling guilt
seeping with relief

as that magic pulled
gently the fragments
of my hostility
from beneath adolescent
skin, breaking
the surface again.

Blackened bark shrouds
the tree at touching
level from the house
fire which blew out all of her
windows in its explosive
birth where seven years
of bad luck rained down
all at once from her
shattered mirror, yet
she still carries
pieces lodged within
from her own begrudging exit
through a collapsed living
room window, refusing
a return to the healing
tree which still thrives
and I wonder how deep
the scarring has worked.

Old Woman in a New Room

"It is as if"
she says
while we sit
in her new unwanted
room in a new
unwanted space
"I have fallen
off the face
of the earth"

and as I watch that tired
old phrase floating
away listlessly from
lips I have just recently discovered
deep grooves in
I let no equally
inexpressive responses
of my own enter
this room

knowing sometimes a tired
old phrase is all a tired
old woman has—
one whose relatives,
not knowing what to say
to someone who has lost
an entire life's history
in a twenty minute housefire,
opt for rushing away from
ashes and black wooden skeletons

and into their own lives
where they can answer
with relief and confidence
when asked "What's new?"
"Oh, not too much."

I silently shake
my head in agreed disgust
with the suddenly old
woman who used to be
my mother
amidst furniture donated
by strangers who read
about us in the newspaper.

the very cold moon

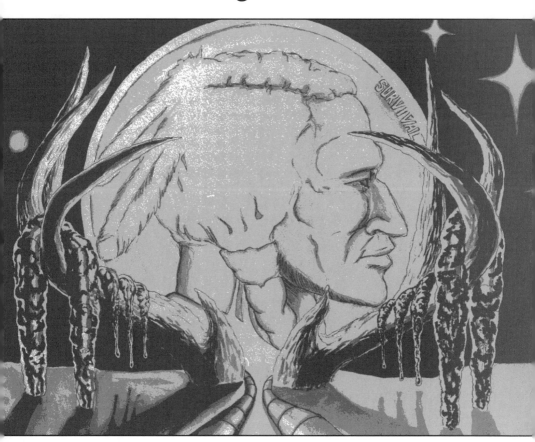

Over Coffee

The grinder cuts through
halting our conversation
forcing us silent
for the moment.

We resume as the brew perks
savoring from the next room
the distinct aroma
carried on breezes

bringing us to
the denial of civilian Auschwitz
the dismissal of civilian America
the scents of death.

My Jewish friend enjoys
the rich flavor
of freshly pulverized beans
until I reveal the grinder's brand name.

He doesn't finish his cup
refusing to use German products
while I drain the dark liquid
envious of that choice of disdain.

Flight

While you sleep again in early isolation somewhere
on the impossibly flat stretch where the arc
of the earth is nearly visible
between Snyder and Lubbock
the pheasant lifts itself from the dead
field to my right and enters my path
nearly greeting my windshield at seventy
more miles per hour than survival would allow
iridescent tail feathers rustling in my wake, this
the first pheasant I have seen since I was seven
the one my cousin released from his hunting
belt, splitting its gut, removing the last steaming
remnants of life with a knife—this I can still smell
if I think hard enough—ripping feathers gleaming dully
in moonlight, the one whose head I secretly took
home and slid under my bed to prevent my relative
from discarding that triumphant crest
in his superior pride, relenting
only when the stench of its passing filled my room
with the truth I could not stop this inevitable process
regardless of my stubborn will, silently removing the skull
and decaying flesh and moving on, as this pheasant does now
setting out on to his own life where I begin
that endless drive I know will bring me back
here to you in some other time and circumstance
hoping we will remain connected if my persistence does
not fail me this time.

Indian Religion at the Turn of the Century

The set of twelve
purple Christmas ornaments—
six light, six dark, my former
Catholic niece commissioned her
Jehovah's Witness friend to bead for her
agnostic uncle is now one dark
fewer, incomplete her Longhouse
daughter shattering one in
a vaguely heavy grasp, cut and fragmented
mirrors falling to the deep
carpet where they leave her child
hands and feet bleeding,
starting this all
over again, with another
indelible stain.

The Old Moccasin Dance Is Sometimes
Not Enough

While we lifted ourselves
in the conference room of a luxury
hotel sitting at the river's edge surrounded
by patronizing smiles of an exclusive island
community, from folding chairs and half
flat cans of Pepsi, moving to the first
disorganized sounds of the Old
Moccasin Dance, driven by a language
we did not understand the meaning of anymore
but could mouth just the same, reduced
to repetition and memory,
other wars were being lost.

At home, your daughter, who last
year by phone told us she missed
us so bad she wanted to be cold with us
when we lied to her to make her new home
seem better, telling her it had dropped
into the negative digits, slept on
your mother's couch disjointed
and disrupted from living five time
zones away from us, in the tropics, though she wanted
to be awake at every moment for the next
two weeks to fit in a year's worth
of time with us.

There, her closed eyes shifted back and forth, like our feet
across this floor, bleeding colors we have only seen
in the full saturation lithograph calendars of Hawaii you bring home
to remind us of the next year you will not be with us,

and when you plead you know the likelihood of our traveling
there is the same as your replanting yourself here, your roots
as blonde and damaged as they are, though for your time here
you dye them back to their natural, horse chestnut brown
a color your progeny barely recognizes, preferring to envision
you with streaks and flows a color the only name we have for as
"reservation smoke shop discount jewelry," but your daughter names
"Sunset Gold," in a place where, even in dreams, she now calls home.

And at the moment we moved back and she pushed forward, less than a
mile from her dozing form, another child slept suddenly, permanently
and dreamless beneath the wheels of a speeding unregistered Indian car
whose driver, a graduate of the reservation school of anger
management, was so enraged, ramming the truck carrying the woman
he saw as his wife for the next seven generations, he did not notice the
tiny form he had dislodged from the truck's bed, a child who had an
hour before gone to the Halloween Haunted House looking for ghosts,
finding herself in their company on a reservation road we have spent
decades walking and you know, the next morning over breakfast
and the news, that we have just missed that car's tires for years
and you check your return flight tickets over coffee.

It Goes Something Like This

I have heard this story
before, she walks alone
her moccasins cracking east
coast sand kernels
along the white-washed Atlantic
City Boardwalk waiting
for the train that will take her
to a school she'd only heard of
that morning, discovering
strangers and a packed bag
with her parents as she came down
for breakfast, and suddenly the midway
music is cut by the more familiar
sounds of home, someone
singing a Tuscarora Social song.
He is dark and she joins in the song
as they, two children, view the ocean
together for the first time.
They board the train and share
a seat the rest of the way
to Carlisle Indian School
and are married as
soon as they graduate.

Many voices have repeated
in the best oral tradition
this story of my grandparents
with great vividness

the beadwork design
in her moccasins
the song he sang
bending my doubting questions silent.
As I start to ask why
they hadn't known
each other on the reservation
or at least seen each other board
or why the New York
to Pennsylvania train stopped
at the New Jersey coastline
I realize they could have met
emptying Headmaster chamberpots
or as voices in black
isolation chambers for speaking
a language still their only link
and I am satisfied with the version
I hear. Sometimes the story is
enough to bring me home.

About the Author

Eric Gansworth is Onondaga and was raised on the Tuscarora Indian Reservation in western New York. He received his associate's degree from Niagara County Community College and his bachelor's and master's degree in English from State University College at Buffalo. His first novel, *Indian Summers*, was published in 1998 by Michigan State University Press. Other work of his, fiction and poetry, has appeared in the anthologies: *Growing Up Native American*; *Blue Dawn, Red Earth*; *Iroquois Voices, Iroquois Visions*; *The Second Word Thursdays Anthology*; and the forthcoming *Children of the Dragonfly*; *Nothing but the Truth: An Anthology of Native American Literature*; and *For Winter Nights: Native American Storytellers*. Work has also been included in the journals: *slipstream*, *phati'tude*, *Blue Line*, *UCLA American Indian Culture and Research Journal*. Gansworth is also a visual artist whose paintings and photographs have been widely exhibited in New York State. Gansworth is an Assistant Professor of English at Niagara County Community College, where he teaches Creative Writing, Freshman Composition, Film as Literature and Native American Literature.